JOHN RUSSELL
POPE
ARCHITECT OF EMPIRE

JOHN RUSSELL
POPE
ARCHITECT OF EMPIRE

STEVEN MCLEOD BEDFORD

Introduction by
WILLIAM L. MACDONALD

With New Photography by
JONATHAN WALLEN

RIZZOLI
NEW YORK

First published in the United States of America in 1998 by
Rizzoli International Publications, Inc.
300 Park Avenue South, New York NY 10010

Library of Congress Cataloging-in-Publication Data

    Bedford, Steven.
        John Russell Pope, architect of empire / Steven
McLeod Bedford ;
    William L. McDonald, introduction ; Jonathan Wallen,
new photography
        p.   cm.
    Includes bibliographical references and index.
    ISBN 0–8478–2086–6
    1. Pope, John Russell, 1874–1937   2. Archi-
tects—United States Biography.   3. Classicism in
architecture—United States.
I.   Title
NA737.P6B43   1998
720' .92—dc21
[B]
                                     97-49820

Designed by ABIGAIL STURGES

Printed and bound in Singapore

CONTENTS

ACKNOWLEDGMENTS

The completion of this book, and the dissertation on which it is based, depended on many kinds of assistance. I am indebted to the financial support provided by my parents and grandparents, without which I would have abandoned this endeavor long ago. Other financial help came from the Graham Foundation, the Smithsonian Institution, and the Department of Art History at Columbia University. I am also indebted to the staffs of Avery Library at Columbia University, AIA Library, the Library of Congress, the Office of Research Support of the Smithsonian Institution, the exhibition and archives staff of the National Gallery of Art, the National Archives, the American Academy in Rome, Yale University Libraries, the Tate Gallery, the British Museum, the Redwood Library, The Huntington Library, the Virginia State Library, and the Alderman Library at the University of Virginia.

Several people were instrumental in helping my research. Tony Wrenn, archivist at the AIA Library was extremely encouraging in the early stages of work, as was Richard Champlin of the Redwood library. Cynthia Field and James Goode of the Smithsonian were especially helpful during my tenure there as a fellow. Ford Peatross and Mary Ison of the Prints and Photographs Division of the Library of Congress suggested new avenues for research. Maygene Daniels and the late Dick Saito opened much of the National Gallery's Archives to me. Sue Kohler of the Commission of Fine Arts was especially helpful as well. The late Diana Wilson guided me through the Huntington Library's holdings on Pope. Janet Parks, Herbert Mitchell, and Angela Giral of Avery worked tirelessly in answering my requests for information. Nancy Matthews of Meridian House not only gave me free rein of the collections there, but also opened her home to me during my visits to Washington. General George Pugh and Michael Sillerman opened their collections to me. Catha Grace Rambusch encouraged me in pursuing this project.

Many have advised me in their areas of expertise: Richard Chafee and David Van Zanten on the École des Beaux-Arts; Christopher Thomas on Henry Bacon; Leslie Boney on the architecture of Wilmington, North Carolina; the late Douglas Gordon on Baltimore society; David Chase on the architecture of Newport, Rhode Island; Elizabeth Grossman on Paul Cret. T. J. Young, Woodward Garber, Alfred Easton Poor, and George Colyer all shared their memories of working for Pope. Jonathan Wallen graciously shared his photographs of Pope buildings with me. Mrs. Jane Ridgeway, Pope's daughter, also granted me access to some of Pope's records.

The late George Collins was my dissertation advisor until his retirement from Columbia in 1985. As a result, Professors Joseph Connors and Alfred Frazer carefully guided me through the long dissertation/book process, patiently reading and revising several drafts. I am also grateful to several others for reading and commenting on various chapters, including Mary Woods, Anne ffolliott, Penny Jones, Carol Willis, Richard Cote, and Gwendolyn Wright. Finally, David Morton of Rizzoli reworked the massive tome of my dissertation into its much more manageable current size. To anyone inadvertently omitted from these lists, I apologize deeply.

Finally, there are personal obligations that I must acknowledge. Laura, my wife, has taken much of her time in the care of our children, Nat and Emma, and put up with my angst over this book and the dissertation that preceded it. I would, however, like to dedicate this book to all those in my life who did not live to see its completion, especially our son Samuel Kerr McLeod Bedford, and Ch. Halcyon Dreadnought, my best friend.

PREFACE

When one looks out from the upper floor of the Hirshhorn Gallery on the south side of the Mall in Washington, D.C., one realizes John Russell Pope's impact on one of America's most important spaces. He was responsible for the removal of the Mall's trees, the design of the National Gallery of Art, the National Archives, the American Pharmaceutical Association, the Jefferson Memorial, and he served as a design critic for the Board of Architectural Consultant's work on the Federal Triangle. As a member of the Commission of Fine Arts, he passed judgment on several projects around the Mall. As briefly outlined by William L. MacDonald, Pope's thirty-four-year career expressed the grandiloquent aspirations of private and public patrons.

In essence Pope's career can be seen as the paradigm for that of the academically trained architect. As the *New York Times* noted in 1937, Pope must be congratulated with "a sincere and reasoned enthusiasm [for] the fine consistency of purpose that animated him throughout his career," i.e. his firm adherence to a belief in the existence of an assemblage of ideal forms that were developed in the distant past and that remained valid as forms expressive of the spirit of the age. This tenacious adherence produced "temples that sit serene in the moil and toil of modern commerce [and] belong to a specific period in our development as a nation: [they] help express and interpret the era through which we have just lived and in which we still strive to come to grips with our national soul."

However, after his death in 1937 interest in Pope virtually ceased. The shifting trends of architectural style condemned his work as retardataire. Major luminaries of modernism, including Joseph Hudnut and William Lescaze, reviled his work, while John Burchard and Albert Bush-Brown, in their AIA-sponsored history of American architecture (1961) found no merit in Pope's work. Consequently, prior to the completion of my dissertation on Pope in 1994 (*The Architectural Career of John Russell Pope,* Columbia University) there were no major studies of Pope's architecture, and virtually no secondary sources for information on Pope's career. The only work on Pope, Royal Cortissoz's *Architecture of John Russell Pope,* was completed in 1930, a full seven years before Pope's death, and it only provides photographs of major commissions.

Studies on Pope are further hampered by the far-flung nature of documents relating to his career. At Pope's death in 1937, his wife, Sadie, on learning that there existed no formal partnership agreement with Eggers and Higgins, virtually emptied the office of her late husband's papers. The papers and effects were stored at the family homes in New York and Newport. A flood in Newport and losses in New York City guaranteed that the records would not survive the death of Sadie in 1976. Many other renderings by Eggers were lost in fires and office moves of the successor firm of Eggers and Higgins. Finally, in the early 1970s, the remaining drawings were dispersed among employees, friends, and clients.

In order to reconstruct Pope's career for my dissertation, I was obliged to use a variety of disparate and distant sources, from interviews of former employees to college transcripts, to archives from Los Angeles to London and Paris, in addition to the usual sources such as contemporary periodicals. The basic research was painfully slow and costly. The discovery of a large cache of photographs of Pope drawings at the Smithsonian Institution completely changed the nature of my work. These several hundred photographs in the Juley Collection provided information on hundreds of barely known commissions. This information further enlarged the scope of the dissertation and required several more rounds of archival research to understand the nature and meaning of the drawings. However, I was then able to reconstruct most of the office's commissions and develop a greater understanding of Pope's approach to design, the inner workings of his office, and the concerns of his clients. Due to the size of the project I did not discuss Pope's designs for cruise ships, yacht commissions, nor any of his decorative art designs.

Over ten years of research and writing culminated in the completion of my Ph.D. dissertation in 1994. This was a massive piece of research, with 570 pages of text and over 300 pages of illustrations. When I was approached by David Morton of Rizzoli to write a book on Pope, it was clear that, in today's commercial market, the cost of producing a book on the scale of my dissertation was prohibitive. As a result the current book has been judiciously pared to a more reasonable size.

With such dramatic reductions come some trade-offs. The original footnotes and bibliography were either eliminated or reduced. The number of buildings discussed was also cut, limited to the most important commissions. In essence this book stands as a distillation of my dissertation. If you desire more text, replete with proper academic apparatus, then you should consult the dissertation. However, this book contains photography that one could not dream of being able to use in a dissertation.

FOREWORD

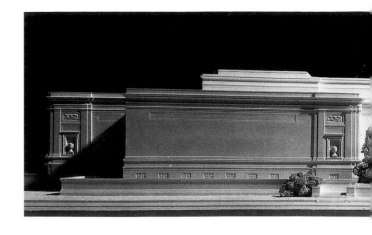

In spite of the prominence of his major works, no solid book about John Russell Pope (1873–1937) has appeared during the sixty years since his death. Now Steven Bedford, having mastered the archival records and a mostly anecdotal and polemical literature, describes Pope's instructive career (as a model Beaux-Arts architect, ed.), analyzes his successes and failures, and provides a sense of the man himself in this first study of a consequential figure in the tangled story of American architecture. His career overlapped the emergence of modernism, when industrial designers transformed familiar, everyday objects. The new architecture, given popular and colorful form at the Chicago Exposition of 1933–34 (the years when John Northrop also designed the epochal DC-2), was spread by those passionately devoted to supplanting traditional buildings with forms for the modern age. Pope, under attack, seemed isolated, marooned, yet his most famous and affective work dates from the 1930s.

Non-classical modes came easily to him. House clients could have almost any style they wanted; his training at the École des Beaux-Arts and in Bruce Price's office served him well. But his efforts in commercial design—few were built—were unsuccessful, save for the Richmond railroad station, and the skyscraper problem defeated him (one project took the form of a forty-story obelisk). Pope's planning schemes, those for the Yale, Johns Hopkins, and Dartmouth campuses, for example, are well conceived, and he contributed to the arrangement of the Rockefeller Center site. Yale rejected most of his sensible ideas but built his Calhoun College and later his Payne Whitney Gymnasium, an impressive work of modernized historicism in its linear clarity and effective massing. Throughout his career Pope was a determined competitor who became ever more disenchanted with his clients. But then, he lived, as architects so often must, with committees, commissions, regulations, improbable programs, special pleading, and, sometimes, serious mischief.

Classical design was his natural domain. Evidence of his experience in Italy recurs throughout his work and in his frequent use of ancient Roman design elements; his trip to Greece was less potent. Charles Follen McKim's insistence on restraint in handling classical ornament was an article of faith. Like most architects of his training and temperament, Pope found precedents and inspiration in eighteenth- and nineteenth-century folios of measured drawings and restorations of ancient buildings, and in his own drawings and photographs made abroad. This is particularly evident in his tombs and memorials. (The study of folio architecture awaits its student.) But his classicizing buildings, save for the Temple of the Scottish Rite, an early work, are neither copies nor revivals.

In time, Pope developed his own classical manner. Roman precedents were applied to his buildings inside and out, but he gave up such models as the Mausoleum at Halicarnassus and the Athenian and Delphic monuments prized by so many neoclassical architects. Nor was he a slave to an individual master such as Bramante or Palladio (not strictly classical but Italian Renaissance architects). With the exception of the Jefferson Memorial, Pope largely abandoned Roman building types—unlike Cass Gilbert in his 1935 Supreme Court building—in favor of his own non-Roman formal statements. And little evidence of Vitruvianism appears in his work other than in column proportions: he was more creative and less wedded to a system than the Vitruvians.

The Jefferson Memorial, repeatedly and understandably linked to the Pantheon, is—except for its similar silhouette and plan outline—not much derived from Hadrian's masterwork, a timeless statement of interiorization absolute, a fully enclosed unitary volume with a single, sky-high light source. Pope's building, executed somewhat cavalierly after his death by his assistants, is ingeniously open to the air, light, and landscape through spacious axial gaps in an intermittent ring wall, in the manner of his earlier Huntington Masoleum. The

National Gallery of Art, Washington, D.C. Model.

doubled rings of columns, their tight Ionic capitals atop unfluted shafts, and the approach to the building, with its flood of steps and massive podium blocks, are pure Pope. Among the innumerable descendants of the Pantheon, in which every liberty has been taken, Pope's may be the most original.

Pope's American Pharmaceutical Association building in Washington, at the west end of Constitution Avenue, is a modest, single-story box (later enlarged by him) decorated only by shallow pilasters and relief sculpture flanking the entrance. Pope had earlier proposed a similar design for a Lincoln birthplace memorial—he often recycled unused projects. The walls left and right are blank, unwindowed, and the whole is bonded with the ground by a prominent entablature; the attic is bare except for a framed inscription. Set atop a broad, sloping lawn, the facade has a touch of modernism that is much more accessible than Paul Cret's glacial modernized classicism of the neighboring Federal Reserve Board headquarters.

The National Archives building is unique. Steven Bedford tracks the steps by which Pope gradually achieved, through repeated simplifications, a powerful image of simple grandeur. A greatly enlarged steel safe, of the kind seen in the country banks of old western films, seems to have been laid face down on the ground and then enclosed, in part, within a wall, the whole being embellished with classical colonnades. The impression of weight and solidity derives not only from the imposing presence of the central block with its immense, superposed attics, but also from the empty walls and Pope's instinctive shortening of the colonnades, revealing the massive reality of the whole.

His Baltimore Museum of Art prefigured somewhat the National Gallery of Art, where monumental presence is achieved by his most effective use of blank walls and by a dramatic entrance system facing the Mall. The stair system is worth study (Pope would have known the grand Roman stairs, such as those behind Santa Maria Maggiore and at San Gregorio Magno); it joins the Museum with the Mall, celebrating an essential association ignored by the newer East Building. Pope's central feature is a reduced Pantheon dome supported on an elegant ring colonnade of green marble centered on an effectively scaled small fountain. Lengthy exterior walls are unfeatured except for terminal blind niches and slightly cut-back panels; these generous expanses are turned by grouped, intersecting pilasters reminiscent of Michelanglo's treatment of the exterior of Saint Peter's. Finished in 1937, the building horrified modernist polemicists, who cried "No more of Pope's Pantheons!," but the National Gallery, like the National Archives building, has stood the test of time.

Pope was called an eclectic, a dinosaur, a man ignorant of the principles of classical design. But at his best he was imaginative and creative, and he extended the possiblities inherent in the classical canon and earned a permanent place in our architectural landscape. As an architect of monumental American buildings, Pope was the last of that long line of classical interpreters that stretches back in an unbroken sequence to the 1790s. Perhaps the Commission of Fine Arts, in calling him in a 1929 report "a great architect," was not entirely wrong.

WILLIAM L. MACDONALD

Washington, D.C.
September 1997

CHAPTER 1

EDUCATION AND EARLY PRACTICE

Fig. 1-1. Design for an aviary, 1893.

From the time of his graduation from Columbia University in 1894, John Russell Pope began to establish himself as an important figure in the American architectural scene. In 1895, he was the simultaneous winner of the McKim Travelling Fellowship and of the first prize awarded by the American School of Architecture in Rome (later the American Academy in Rome). After eighteen months in Rome, he left to enter the École des Beaux-Arts in Paris, where he was extremely successful. Pope returned to New York in 1900, and after several years in the office of Bruce Price, began his own practice. He then began a thirty-four year career during which he lent expression to the grandiloquent aspirations of private and public patrons. His domestic and monumental architecture established him as a leader in the development of a highly refined and restrained classicism that came to distinguish American architecture from that of its European counterparts.

John Russell Pope was formally educated in the manner typical of many university-trained American architects of his time. There are few surprises in the general make-up of his education. However, it appears that the repertoire of neoclassical forms Pope learned during his training served as a foundation and source of inspiration, and remained the primary component of his design vocabulary until his death. Pope seemed to adhere to the precept that a certain set of classical forms and plans existed whose inherent beauty was immutable.

Pope was born in 1873 into an era during which culture was used as a "disciplining education for the turbulent urban populace." New York in the 1870s and 1880s was a place of nascent cultural cosmopolitanism. The American Museum of Natural History had been founded in 1869. The Astor and Lenox Libraries opened to the public in the 1870s, while the Metropolitan Museum of Art, with its extensive collection of plaster casts of classical sculpture, fragments of architectural ornament, and models, opened in 1872 and moved into its Fifth Avenue building in 1880.

The facts concerning Pope's earliest artistic training are elusive. His father, John Pope (1820–1881), was a competent and successful portrait painter who had studied under Thomas Couture in Paris and had also traveled in Italy. His sitters included abolitionist preacher Henry Ward Beecher, Secretary of War Edward McMasters Stanton, and actor Edwin Booth. A frequent exhibitor at the National Academy of Design, he was made an Associate of the Academy in 1859. His studio appears to have been at home, where young John Russell could have watched and learned directly from him. Mary Avery Pope (born Loomis), the elder John Pope's second wife, was a piano teacher and a landscape painter who also exhibited regularly at the Academy before her son's birth. In such an actively artistic household, it would be difficult for a young man to avoid being exposed to the principles of drawing and composition. John Russell Pope certainly must have visited the exhibitions at the National Academy of Design, for the family house and studio at 49 East Twenty-first Street was only a few blocks away from the Academy building on Twenty-third Street at Fourth Avenue. It is difficult to imagine that he did not go to the Metropolitan Museum or the Museum of Natural History regularly.

EDUCATION

Young Pope's early formal education appears to have been unremarkable. He attended P.S. 35 on New York City's East Side. Education in New York's grammar schools at the time consisted primarily of lectures and rote recitation, the basics of a curriculum that had barely changed since the 1850s. There was little in the regular educational program that might have stimulated Pope's interest in architecture, but he was probably enrolled in a supplementary course in drawing that was offered to the better students. Such a class would have reinforced

Examination May 31, 1893.

John Russell Pope.

11

the importance of what Pope had learned at home and perhaps furthered his grounding in the principles of drawing. He completed this phase of his education in 1888, at the age of fifteen.

At the time he entered college, Pope had no intention of becoming an architect, and his early academic record proves this. After his father's death in 1880, Pope apparently came under the influence of his uncle, Dr. Alfred Loomis, an extremely successful physician, and the young man naturally expressed an interest in becoming a doctor. In the fall of 1888, he entered the sub-freshman class at the City College of New York (CCNY) with the intention of studying medicine. In his first year, however, following a required curriculum, he attained his highest grade in drawing. In his freshman year, again he received his highest marks in drawing. In his sophomore year, consistent with his announced intention of pursuing a career in medicine, Pope chose to follow the scientific, rather than the "classical," curriculum. But again, true to form, he attained the first rank in his drawing course, but he still had not officially professed any interest in architecture.

At CCNY, it was assumed that drawing was an essential component in the curriculum of any well-educated person. Before widespread use of the camera, this skill was crucial for visual communication. Under the tutelage of Salomon Woolf, Pope followed a series of courses of increasing difficulty in the same manner as an architecture student. In his sub-freshman year, he drew in outline from flat and round objects, studied surface shading with crayon, learned elementary perspective, and drew human, geometrical, architectural, and other forms. As a freshman, the course focused on graphic solutions to problems in descriptive geometry, carpentry, machinery, and architecture. He also received further instruction in tinting, shades and shadows, and perspective.

In his sophomore year, his class became more difficult and more typically academic in its approach to instruction in drawing, and Pope began sketching from plaster casts. The examples available at CCNY included the frieze of the Parthenon, the *Venus de Milo,* the *Apollo Belvedere,* and works by Michelangelo, Thorvaldson, and Cellini. In addition, Pope drew from photographs of ancient structures and sites as well as modern European buildings. These models provided Pope with a strong basis for building further drawing skills and forced him to become conversant with classical forms and composition early in his training.

Columbia College

It was Pope's intention to leave CCNY after his sophomore year in order to enter the medical program at The Johns Hopkins University in Baltimore, but after observing a surgical operation, he had a change of heart. Instead, he remained in New York, entering the architecture program at the School of Mines, Columbia College, as a sophomore in 1891.

The curriculum of the architecture program was under the constant scrutiny of its director, William Robert Ware. Ware's pedagogical approach adhered to the prevailing principles of instruction in design: the basis of the entire curriculum was one of classic academicism—the instillation in the minds of students the concept that certain forms were innately, inherently, and immutably beautiful. Ware's definition of the classically beautiful was quite catholic, however, and he exposed his students not only to classical forms but also to medieval and American colonial forms. In addition, he attempted to keep his faculty and favored students abreast of current architectural trends by sending them to experience such events as the 1893 World's Columbian Exposition in Chicago and arranging for the acquisition of a complete set of working drawings of the various exposition buildings.

As a second-year student under Frank Dempster Sherman, Pope learned the elements of architecture in a course whose syllabus read like the table of contents of Ware's *American Vignola.* Beginning with the study of the classical orders, Sherman led his students through exercises on proportion and the use of other architectural elements such as arches, arcades, roof types, and wall treatments. Pope's course in modern architectural history under Talbot Hamlin, which used Leon Palustre's *Architecture de la Renaissance* as its text, glorified French and Italian Renaissance forms. As an adjunct to this course, students were required to draw historically significant structures and elements from photographs and printed illustrations and to reconstruct them based on a verbal description. This exercise linked the courses that taught the orders and elements of architecture and the courses in design, and it demonstrated to students the historical solutions to various building problems they would later confront.

In Professor Maximillian Kress's German archeology course, students read Ernst Kroker's *Katechismus der Archäologie.* It covered all aspects of ancient art, beginning with Egyptian, and provided the student with images and elementary explanations of major monuments such as the Pantheon and the Arch of Constantine in Rome, the Temple of Vesta in Tivoli, the Athenian Acropolis, and the Mausoleum at Halicarnassus, all of which Pope would later use as models for his own building designs. In conjunction with this course, Pope also was required to draw capitals and other architectural ornament, Greek house plans, and the rock-cut tombs of Egypt and Asia Minor.

In the third year, when the newly developed course in architectural engineering was introduced into the curriculum under professors Frank Dempster Sherman and Grenville Snelling, historical studies were still predominant, and in addition, Professor Hamlin's course began to cover oriental ornament.

Given Ware's typically American disdain for theory, one can assume that Pope was exposed only very generally to the works of theoreticians such as Ruskin, Viollet-le-Duc, Gottfried Semper, Quatremère de Quincy, the Blondels, Vitruvius, and Palladio.

The third-year course called Practice was primarily concerned with the development of an ideal building specification that would serve as a model for written building specifications called for in professional practice. The effect of this training on Pope's later work can be seen in his own specifications, wherein he would go to great lengths to ensure that his directions were properly understood.

Two of Pope's designs from 1893 survive. The first presents an aviary constructed of glass with vaguely Saracen metal arches and designed in an oriental style, a mode that would have been covered in the course (fig. 1-1). The parti for the aviary seems to be based on the garden of the Villa Giulia in Rome, which has, however, been reversed, creating a rather awkward spatial organization. Since Pope had received high marks for his drawing work at CCNY, one would have expected him to possess superior skills. In fact, this was not the case. Although fully developed conceptually, the quality of the aviary scheme's draftsmanship is rather poor, and is what one might expect of an early student work. The line work is loose, tentative, and imprecise, even in the rendition of simple iron columns. The applied washes are uneven in color and poorly controlled in placement, giving the work a muddy appearance overall.

The second drawing, for a column commemorating a naval battle, is closely patterned after the column in the Place Vendôme in Paris (fig. 1-2) and is much more competently rendered than the oriental aviary. The quality of the young Pope's draftsmanship, however, may reflect something of Ware's attitude toward presentation and drawing, which he considered secondary to composition. Consequently, there was no reason to expect Pope to produce anything more than competent drawings during his undergraduate years.

Pope performed extremely well in his fourth year. To complete the requirements for his degree, he had to submit a final project, a design for a casino. All evidence of this work is lost, but the design must have been excellent, for Pope's work was chosen for exhibition at the Architectural League's Annual Exhibition in 1894. Although Pope received his bachelor of philosophy degree in architecture in June 1894, postgraduate studies were an absolute necessity. To become a competent architect required more training than the college could provide.

In the summer of 1894, Pope traveled to Intervale, New Hampshire, to work as an assistant to Ware. This trip ensured Ware's continued influence over

Pope and signals the high regard in which Pope held his first mentor's opinions. Pope returned to Columbia College that fall and again worked as Ware's assistant. During this time, Pope may also have been employed by Bruce Price, but no documentation exists because Price's office records have been destroyed.

Fig. 1-2. Design for a commemorative column, 1893.

Rome and the Grand Tour

Pope's education continued with the study of the great architectural monuments of Europe—an essential component of an architect's training. In the spring of 1895, Pope entered the competitions for the McKim Travelling Fellowship and the Rome Prize offered by the American School of Architecture in Rome. Both programs specified the design of a savings bank following the stylistic precedents of the Italian or French Renaissance, and based on the functional program and site plan of McKim, Mead & White's recently completed Bowery Savings Bank.

Fig. 1-3. Design for a savings bank (entry for both McKim Travelling Fellowship and Rome Prize), 1895.

When the Travelling Fellowship jury met to judge the finished competition drawings, Pope's design was selected (fig. 1-3). A few weeks later, the American School jurors met and the same design again won. It was, according to juror Frank Miles Day, "so distinctly superior to all the others that the jury had not the slightest doubt as to the correctness of its decision."

Pope's mode of presentation for the bank program was in the manner of an *envoi* (a sketch dispatched by a student to a Master) *de Rome* of a French *Grand Prix pensionnaire* (student recipient of a stipend). The drawings, all orthographic projections, were carefully rendered with ink washes, creating an authoritative image. His chief rivals opted for more picturesque methods of depiction. Pope's decision to follow the French model was a well-calculated one, for the jury was predominantly French-trained and his chosen method of presentation emulated the style that had set the standard for measured drawings of antique buildings. Pope's mastery of this method convinced the jurors that he possessed the technical skills necessary to profit from measuring the monuments of Italy and Greece.

Pope's submission was up-to-date in its classical borrowing. Reflecting America's newfound obsession with the classical, the elevation of the bank is clearly based on Charles Atwood's Fine Arts Pavilion at the World's Columbian Exposition. Not only had Pope seen the building, but he could have studied

the design in depth from the drawings at Columbia. The Ionic arcade, furthermore, closely resembles that of Bruce Price's American Surety Building (1894–96), which Pope surely knew. Pope's winning drawings were exhibited at the annual Department of Architecture exhibition.

On the other hand, Pope was unsure of his own ability to profit from an extended trip to Europe, and had hoped to have completed his master's degree before leaving for Rome. In early June, he requested that his award be deferred for a year. Ware supported Pope's request to delay the departure in a letter to the president of Columbia College, but the issue proved to be a volatile one. First of all, Ware's support of Pope was not entirely unselfish. Ware would lose a trained assistant in his studio and would probably be unable to replace him in time for the fall semester. He was certainly aware that his students were insufficiently trained in the principles of construction and the preparation of contract documents. But in this case, Pope was also being used as a tool in an on-going educational feud between McKim and Ware. McKim considered Rome and Greece the primary sources of good architecture, while Ware believed that foreign study should include the northern countries and the Gothic. By keeping Pope under his wing, Ware was able to frustrate McKim's efforts to completely control the program of the fledgling academy. Upon receiving the president's assent to delay Pope's departure, Ware

wrote to McKim to seek the approval of the trustees of the American School of Architecture in Rome. McKim and the other founders of the school were furious and refused to agree. Richard Morris Hunt denounced Pope's request, saying it would interfere with the tenure of the subsequent year's prize winner. In addition, it would look very awkward for a Rome Prize winner to defer the award, as that would imply that more educational benefit could be derived from a year in New York than a year in Rome. McKim and the other founders of the school were steadfast in their insistence that Pope leave for Rome in the fall of 1895, and by August, Pope had agreed, finally arriving in Rome on 15 October.

The schedule that Pope and his colleagues followed while in Rome was vaguely modeled on the French academic program. Six months were to be spent studying, measuring, and drawing the monuments of antiquity and the Renaissance, while the next four were to be spent in travel and study according to a plan approved by the resident director of the school, Austin Lord, in conjunction with McKim.

Because financial matters were a problem for the young school, McKim came over in December 1895 to assess the state of the institution. He also directly supervised the students there and advised them about places to visit. He was very specific in prescribing the appropriate monuments for his young charges, urging them to study the remains of ancient Rome, followed by further exposure to the works of Bramante,

Peruzzi, the Sangallo family, and Vignola. One can only imagine the forceful impression created by McKim leading his small group of students through the streets of Rome in search of his favorite buildings.

By 4 May 1896, the American *pensionnaires* had just completed six weeks in Greece and were finishing work at the Acropolis, where Pope measured the Erectheum and the Propylaea. He used a homemade version of a pantograph, with which he produced exact full-size details of these monuments. By 15 June the group had worked in Sicily, the Peloponnisos, Corinth, and Naples, and had just returned from Pompeii, where Pope had measured a Roman villa then called the Casa Nuova. (Attempts to determine the modern name of this villa have proved fruitless.) Pope later turned these measurements into an *envoi*. The drawing style that Pope employed in producing these *envois* seems to reflect his lack of confidence: they are hard-edged, mechanical, and lightly drawn.

In the final months of 1896, Pope undertook a brief tour through northern Italy. Traveling first to Siena, he measured the entrance to the library of the cathedral and the Palazzo Pellini. In Perugia, only the Udienza del Cambio seemed to catch his eye. In Pistoia, during the last few days of August he sketched the churches of San Giovanni and San Andrea (fig. 1-4). In Florence, the Palazzo Vecchio, the Library of San Lorenzo, and the Duomo were visited and recorded in September, along with, in Venice, the monument to the condottiere Bartolomeo

acterized by broad, bold strokes with little evidence of correction or erasure. His sketch of the Duomo in Florence (fig. 1-6) is probably the best example of his work during this time. He turned his set of sketches of the Colleoni monument into an *envoi* that demonstrates the increased refinement of his technical skills. The washes are clear and crisp, and the architectural elements and decoration are rendered with a bold hand, while the depiction of the equestrian statue strongly conveys the three-dimensional nature of the subject.

A few of Pope's sketches bore the notation "see photograph," indicating the beginning of a long-term interest in photography, which would have such appeal that Pope would later abandon his sketchbooks for a large-format camera. On other drawings, color notes were written, a typically American technique. During his travels, Pope also produced a few watercolor sketches in a rapid, painterly manner with an evenness of color value that tends to flatten the volume of the structure depicted.

It was during these early years in Europe that Pope began to compile a large inventory of the classical forms that would later appear in his work. He thus began to define a drawing style that could be characterized as idiosyncratic within the academic manner. Almost all of the surviving images from 1895 to 1896 are objective pencil elevations that record buildings in a restrained classical manner. However, his free application of notes on color as well as the general style of his watercolors demonstrate a slightly romantic countercurrent in his work. When the Academy drawings were exhibited at the Metropolitan Museum of Art in 1899, Pope's drawings of the Casa Nuova in Pompeii were singled out as being among the most important in the *New York Times*.

École des Beaux-Arts

By the end of 1896, Pope was in Paris to begin the final episode in his twelve years of formal architectural education. He entered the *atelier preparatoire* of Godefroy and Freynet, a choice probably influenced by the fact that some of his classmates from Columbia had used this atelier to prepare for their entrance exams at the École des Beaux-Arts.

Most of the exams tested knowledge of mathematics and perspective and skill in drawing; only one, the *concours d'admission*, presented the students with a minor design problem. Developed by Julien Guadet, professor of architectural theory, it called for the design of an entry to a children's hospital. Pope chose as his parti a barrel vault flanked by coffered, trabeated passageways (fig. 1-7). This is exactly the same parti used in the Hôtel des Monnaies in Paris, the Palazzo Farnese in Rome, and Leon Vaudoyer's Conservatoire des Arts et Métier, all later illustrated in Guadet's *Eléments et théorie de*

Fig. 1-5. Rendering of the monument to Bartolomeo Colleoni, Venice, Italy, 1896.

Colleoni (fig. 1-5) and the church of Santa Maria Della Salute, the tomb of Dante in Ravenna, the cathedral in Orvieto, the Palazzo Communale in Bologna, and brickwork details in Rimini.

Pope's sketches, watercolors, and renderings were focused on Romanesque, Gothic, and Renaissance structures. Not one depicted a classical monument. It seems that he followed Ware's advice of producing an eclectic visual sampler of buildings, and chose to illustrate details more than complete building forms, indicating that he was more interested in decorative elements than general massing and scale. It also seems that he believed Rome gave him all the necessary models for the massing and large-scale composition of buildings, while northern Italy provided the models for decorative elements and furnishings.

In general, the drawing technique shifted away from the stiff, self-conscious technique of his earlier work to show a stronger, more confident hand char-

l'architecture. This choice was probably a calculated move, since Pope had the opportunity to learn the partis favored by Guadet from his lectures. Pope's design obviously met with success, for not only was he admitted to the second class, but he placed second among the competitors.

Pope then entered the atelier of Henry Deglane and immediately set to work on the compulsory examinations and *éléments analytiques*. He probably entered this particular atelier for two reasons: first, because several of his classmates from Columbia were there, and second, because Deglane had just been awarded the commission for the Grand Palais of the Paris Exposition of 1900 and had received a great deal of press.

By October 1897, Pope had passed three of the five required examinations; he had prepared the two required *analytiques*; and he had begun to practice for other projects in the first class. He devoted the rest of 1897 and the first eight months of 1898 to the completion of three *projets rendus*. He also re-

ceived high marks for his final two compulsory scientific exercises, a *Troisième Medaille* for his construction project, and credit for his drawing, modeling, ornamental design, and architectural history exercises in rapid succession between February and June 1898. By August 1898, sixteen months after he had entered the École, Pope had amassed twenty-four *valeurs* and was promoted to the first class. He was the first in his class to be promoted, and thus received the Prix Jean Leclaire for his effort.

In the next sixteen months, Pope continued to work at a feverish pace, and became known for spontaneity and skill in the presentation of his designs, especially the sketch problems *(esquisses)*. One of his *esquisses*, that for an entry to a convent, was retained by the École and has thus survived (fig. 1-8). Here Pope's progress as a draftsman is immediately evident. The free lines of the perspective view flow into unity with the plan and elevation, and the technique is vigorous, expressing an uncommon vitality. Surprising as well is his choice of style for the building,

Fig. 1-6. Sketch of the Duomo, Florence, Italy, 1896.

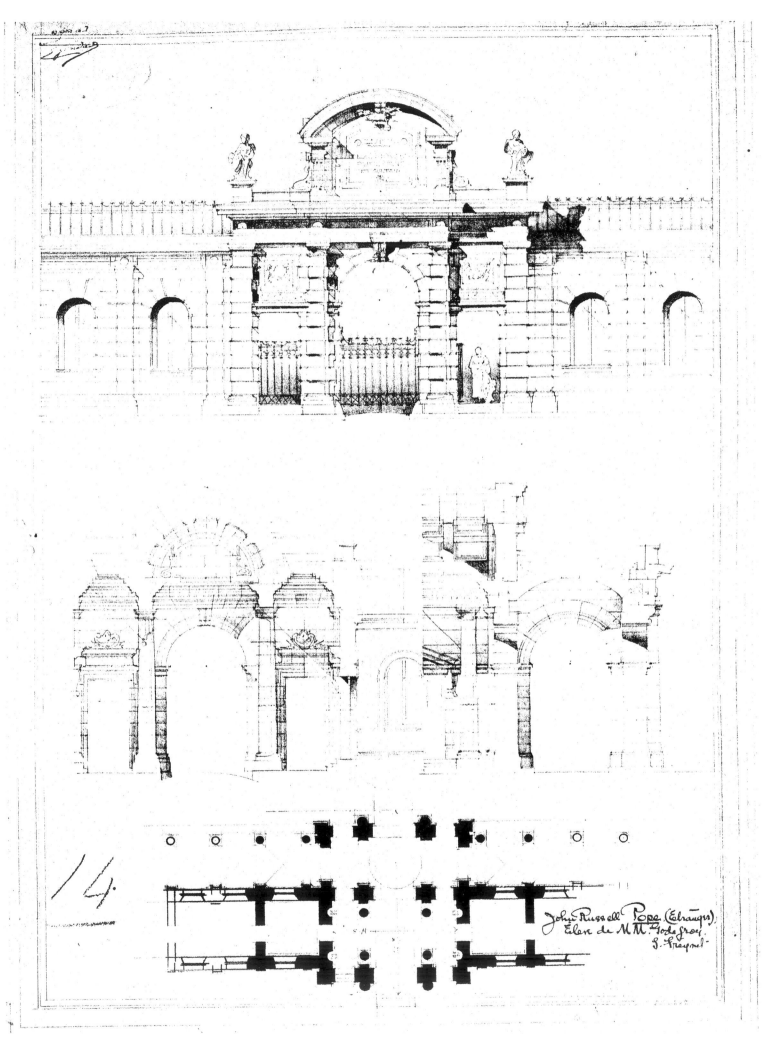

Fig. 1-7

whose romantic, medievalizing forms are carefully governed by the underlying principles of symmetrical composition and axial planning.

Of the remaining three competitions, two were exercises, one each in drawing and modeling; the third was the *Concours d'histoire de l'architecture*. This last competition, for the restoration of the wells in the cloister of the hospital of St. Jean d'Angers, for which Pope received a *Première Seconde Medaille*, is the second and final one from which any visual record survives (fig. 1-9). The method of presentation is much more romantic than any drawing seen previously from his hand, but such a composition is appropriate for the subject. The plan, elevation, and perspective are integrated into a unified vertical composition. The worm's-eye view of the well establishes a context for the object and provides an excellent view of the major facade of the structure, while the side elevation and plan flow out of the foliage surrounding the perspective. The success of the composition is most evident when it is compared to the entry by another American, Albert Nash, of the atelier Pascal. Nash's composition is overly stiff, and his attempt to integrate the various views through the use of a sweeping curved line is unconvincing.

By early 1900, Pope had accumulated more than enough *valeurs* to begin his diploma problem, but several events prevented him from staying on in Paris. The terms of the McKim Fellowship, from which he was then benefitting, would have required his return to Rome by June 1899. However, the American School of Architecture in Rome had by then become the American Academy, and no longer accepted visiting scholars other than its own fellows. Pope enjoyed the confusion by staying on in Paris until the terms of both of his fellowships had run out, but due to a lack of funds, he was then forced to return to the United States in January 1900 before his last *concours* was judged.

Though he had to return before achieving a *grand succès*, Pope's European sojourn had been beneficial in developing his confidence and skills. He had cultivated an ability to solve formulaically complex problems in a very short period of time and then to transmit this information very effectively through his sketches and *projets rendus*. These skills are essentially the sort necessary to run a successful office, and within five years of his return to the United States, he was doing just that.

APPRENTICESHIPS

Pope returned from France at the perfect moment to begin a career as a proponent of the "academic reaction." The American economy was at the height of a

Fig. 1-8

Fig. 1-9

Fig. 1-7. Concours d'admission, *École des Beaux-Arts.*

Fig. 1-8 Esquisse *for entry to a convent*, École des Beaux-Arts.

Fig. 1-9 Concours d'histoire de l'architecture *("Restoration of the wells in the cloister of the hospital of St. Jean d'Anger")*, École des Beaux-Arts.

twenty-five-year period of expansion and consolidation. The continental frontier was officially closed and cities were growing rapidly. Wealth was accumulating in New York at an exponential rate. In the architectural profession, the call for a uniform classicism, already sounded before Pope's departure for Europe, had virtually triumphed, creating a perfect climate for the designer who could provide grand monuments for a newly powerful America. McKim, in summarizing the requirements for success in this milieu, contended in the *American Architect and Building News* of 20 December 1902 that "great opportunities demand thorough training. Confidence comes not from inspiration but from knowledge. The architect who would build for the ages to come must have the training of the ages that are past." With five years of direct contact with the paradigms for America's new classicism, Pope could certainly claim to have satisfied McKim's prerequisites for architectural success.

McKim, Mead & White

Some have suggested that Pope worked for McKim, Mead & White, but the firm's employment records never mention him. It is known that McKim nevertheless did proffer some work. On 31 January 1900, McKim asked Pope, who was apparently ill, if he would be willing to prepare on a freelance basis, under White's supervision, the formal rendered plans for the development of Belle Isle in Detroit. White had already sketched out a scheme that featured a huge Doric column framed at the base by a colonnade, topped with a tripod fueled by natural gas, and illuminated by electric beacons. Having spent a great deal of time on the project, White was apparently anxious to turn the development of his sketches over to someone else to reduce costs. He also needed help to meet a deadline that was only a fortnight away. Given his previous relationship with McKim, Pope probably took the job. Furthermore, his later competition entries for the Monument on the Great Lakes (1905) and, in Ohio, the Perry Memorial (1912) borrowed heavily from the Detroit scheme, lending further circumstantial evidence to support the case that Pope worked for White. In working for White, he would have been exposed to what has been described as the most carefully composed and detailed work of White's career. Pope's subsequent ability to synthesize McKim, Mead & White's dignified borrowings from Renaissance and Roman sources with his own form of monumental classicism surely required an extensive and intimate prior knowledge of the firm's work, which could only have come from working in the office. Despite the fact that the Detroit project was never built, Pope would have been exposed to the elemental sobriety that typified the firm's work in the first decade of this century.

Bruce Price

Whatever his experience with McKim, Mead & White, Pope went on to work for Bruce Price later in 1900. Even if he had not already worked for Price as a student, he would anyway have been attracted to the firm. Price had by this time attained the zenith of his architectural career, but had limited his involvement in the design process, and Pope's decision to enter the firm may have been further influenced by this, for it offered a young designer opportunities for increased authority. Another reason for Pope to join Price was that the latter had built a house for Pope's uncle, Alfred Loomis, in Ringwood, New Jersey (1887), thereby establishing a family connection to the firm.

Since the office records of Price's firm have disappeared, it is impossible to determine with certainty what Pope's role might have been. But given Price's apparent withdrawal from design work, such responsibility may have fallen to Pope. However, the issue is confused by the fact that Pope joined the firm at the same time as Jules Henri de Sibour, an architect who later became known for his flamboyant designs of Washington residences. Samuel Graybill, Price's biographer, noted (in an unpublished doctoral dissertation, Yale University, 1957) a surprising change in Price's work following the arrival of Pope and De Sibour. The designs produced by the firm after 1900 reflected dichotomous trends, one being a restrained classicism, and the other a more exuberant and flamboyant adaptation of the eclectic modern French style. Using the later work of these two architects as a guide, one can certainly distinguish De Sibour's aggressively eclectic designs from Pope's restrained and severe classicism.

The first project that Pope may have participated in was the Georgian House for Seven Thousand Dollars, designed for the October 1900 issue of *Ladies' Home Journal* (fig. 1-10). Although one would expect a house of such low cost to be decorated simply, the severity of the design seems more characteristic of Pope's later work than Price's previous work, and available illustrations do not carry any indication of authorship. The interior plan is unassuming and direct, as one would expect in a building with few rooms. Additional evidence that Pope was involved in this project is found in his "moonlighting" work. In 1901, almost immediately after the publication of the design, Pope produced a Georgian house for Professor Willard Humphreys in Princeton (figs. 1-11, 1-12). With the exception of the addition of eyebrow dormers on the side elevations, the house (destroyed by fire in 1904) exactly corresponds to the published Georgian house in plan and elevation. In order for Pope to have produced such a set of drawings, he must have been involved in the design of the *Ladies' Home Journal* project.

Fig. 1-10

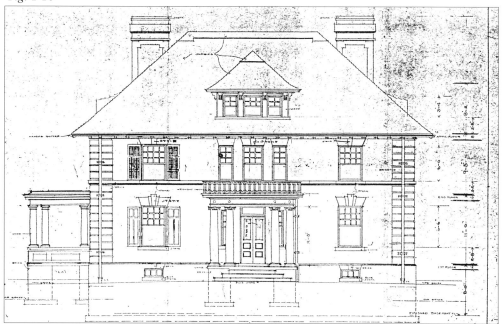

Fig. 1-11

Fig. 1-10. Ladies' Home Journal *Georgian House for Seven Thousand Dollars, 1900.*

Figs. 1-11, 1-12. Willard Humphreys house, Princeton, New Jersey, 1901. Elevation and plan.

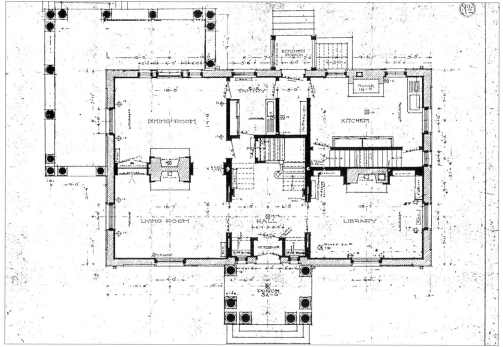

Fig. 1-12

21

Fig. 1-13

Fig. 1-14

Fig. 1-13. George St. George house, Tuxedo Park, New York, c. 1900.

Fig. 1-14. Howard house, Washington, D.C., 1907.

In 1901, Price's office was also designing an additional mansion known as Kingscote on the Charles Gould estate in Lakewood, New Jersey, for Gould's son Kingdon. The exterior of the house was rectilinear and formally severe in the same manner as Pope's later work. It was essentially an elaboration of the *Ladies' Home Journal* project. The porches of the suburban house became porticoes, while the ground-floor windows were converted to French doors. The interior layout was an open, axial plan in which a large entrance hall was crossed by a narrow hallway that allowed the visitor to understand the entire ground floor arrangement immediately. Although the same plan had already been used by Price at Georgian Court (1899), the main house on the Gould estate, its later use by Pope in many of his country house designs suggests that Pope was involved in the design of Kingscote.

Following a similar line of reasoning, the George St. George house (c. 1900, fig. 1-13) in Tuxedo Park, New York, can be attributed to Pope. The severity of the colonial revival form would be the primary link to Pope. Aside from similar style, the St. George house, built on a grander scale than the Kingdon Gould house, also shares certain design similarities with it, most notably its elemental massing and use of exaggerated quoins, indicating a common designer. Again, these decorative traits were familiar elements of Pope's later houses. Finally, as with the Gould family, Pope would receive a later commission for the Tuxedo Club (begun 1927) from the St. Georges.

Two subsequent commissions were also probably designed by Pope: the Perrin house (1902) and the Howard house (1907, fig. 1-14), both in Washington, D.C. The houses, situated within a block of one another on Sixteenth Street, were sober and severe

and simple in plan). Both were excellent interpretations of the Georgian revival style.

Pope surely worked on two conservative public buildings designed by Price's office during this period. The first, the Washington County Library (1900–1901) in Hagerstown, Maryland (fig. 1-15), possessed a raw sobriety. The motif of an arched pediment supported by Ionic columns *in antis* was later used by Pope in a study for the Frick Collection in New York and in several of his country house designs. The final project in Pope's collaboration with the Price firm dates from after Price's death in May 1903. This was the competition for the Freedman's Hospital (1904–08) in Washington, D.C. (fig. 1-16). On 3 March 1905, Price's firm was selected from among twenty entries.

Completed in 1908, the hospital was an essay in the stark, late-Georgian style. A shallow Ionic portico was flanked by ranges of windows with projecting surrounds, while a saucer-shaped dome rose slightly above a stepped parapet, breaking the cubic and horizontal emphasis of the design. The sobriety of the forms complemented the simple volume of the structure and added to the severe, monumental impact of the hospital. In this design one sees Pope's first experimentation with a domical parti, a motif he would continue to explore and refine throughout his career.

PROFESSIONAL PRACTICE

Pope started practicing on his own in 1905, but he had already established a separate professional identity following Price's death. In November 1903, he applied for membership in the American Institute of

Architects (AIA), sponsored by McKim, who had just left office as its president, and the Architectural League of New York, seeking institutional seals of approval from organizations that were much more selective then than they are today.

Like most young architects, Pope initially won few commissions. To supplement his income, he returned to teaching, and in the summer of 1905 was invited to assist McKim in one of the two newly formed ateliers of the Columbia School of Architecture.

The question of what McKim actually taught has never been answered adequately, but it is known that he offered little as a teacher. In his quest to create a national style appropriate to the newfound energy and confidence of the nation, McKim promoted a particular brand of historicism that was ultimately based on the forms of the Italian Renaissance and republican and imperial Rome. But beyond absorbing McKim's belief in the ascendancy of certain styles

and taking up the search for a national style, Pope had little to learn from such a teacher. Pope himself became an excellent teacher within the context of the atelier system at Columbia.

From 1905 onward, Pope's residential clientele slowly increased. Most of his commissions were for large country houses whose owners demanded antique European furnishings and stained glass, obliging Pope to travel to Europe on a number of occasions on buying trips. Despite the interruptions, Pope remained an instructor at the atelier under McKim's relaxed supervision until the summer of 1907, when the demands of practice forced his resignation from teaching, thus ending his apprenticeship and finally freeing him from any direct contact with his mentors.

By the time Pope resigned from his academic appointment in 1907, his practice was already quite active. He had completed several large residential commissions, had extensive residential work "on

Fig. 1-15

Fig. 1-16

Fig. 1-15. Washington County Library, Hagerstown, Maryland, 1900–1901.

Fig. 1-16. Freedman's Hospital, Washington, D.C., 1904–08.

Fig. 1-17. Sketch for Baltimore Museum of Art, c. 1926–27.

the boards," and was involved in competitions for major public buildings. His practice had even grown to the point where he needed several employees.

A great emphasis was placed on the quality and beauty of all the drawings in Pope's office, from grand renderings to simple construction documents. In the earliest years, all the drawings were made by Pope himself, but as work increased, he had to convey his designs and standards to others so that they could bring a greater volume of work to the same level. Consequently, he developed a method of disseminating his ideas that drew upon the best aspects of his drafting abilities as well as his skills as a critic. The development of a design beyond the sketch to the rendering stage was a laborious process for Pope: he lacked the technical virtuosity of a professional renderer or construction document detailer. Pope preferred instead to focus his energies on the design aspects of the project.

In developing a design, Pope would first take a good deal of time to conceptualize the whole design, and would then follow a method learned during his days at the École and borrowed from the *esquisse* stage of a competition. He would first sketch out the plan and elevation for a new project on small-ruled paper in a very simple freehand line drawing, and then turn these sketches over to an assistant for development (fig. 1-17). As the design was developed, Pope would criticize it in the manner of a *patron* at the École, while the assistant continued to elaborate the design according to Pope's recommendations. The final design was then developed into elegant renderings and perspectives by Pope or his assistants.

The drawings of the Jacobs house (1901–03) in Newport, Rhode Island provide further information about Pope's early design process (figs. 1-18, 1-19). There is evidence of numerous erasures and alterations in plan, confirming the observation that Pope took a long time to develop a design fully, either on his own or in consultation with his client. Just as he had done in his student sketches, instead of drawing to illustrate his intentions, he used written notes to describe the style of each room, indicating a very loose approach to controlling the design of the interior.

This general working method allowed Pope to concentrate his efforts on the essential elements of the design without becoming bogged down in the details himself. By the mid 1920s, with many country house and public commissions to his credit or underway, much of the detail work and client contact was left to employees, which had the effect of distancing Pope both from the final product and his clients. This would be interpreted as arrogance and snobbishness, but actually may have reflected the lack of self-confidence that had already been observed during his student days. This seeming reticence may have been an exaggerated manifestation of an office manner according to which employer and employee maintained a very formal relationship. However, Pope's refusal to meet with clients he did not like, or who were not prestigious enough, placed a great burden on his employees, as they had to assume considerable responsibility while Pope remained in the background. Pope was not, however, discourteous to his clients; he simply preferred not to develop any sort of personal relationship with most of them.

When Otto R. Eggers (1882–1964) joined the firm in 1909, Pope acquired a promising delineator who would become one of America's greatest renderers, and a relationship began that eventually led to an informal partnership. In collaboration with Eggers, Pope continued to design almost all of his most well-known structures, but virtually ceased producing finished drawings.

Eggers, like Pope, was born in Manhattan. He attended public schools in Greenwich Village before entering the firm of Elliot Lynch, while studying architecture part-time at the Cooper Union and in the Hornbostel atelier of the Beaux-Arts Institute of Design. His greatest innovation in architectural rendering was in the use of the airbrush to lay down washes that built like a glazed surface to create vibrant blue

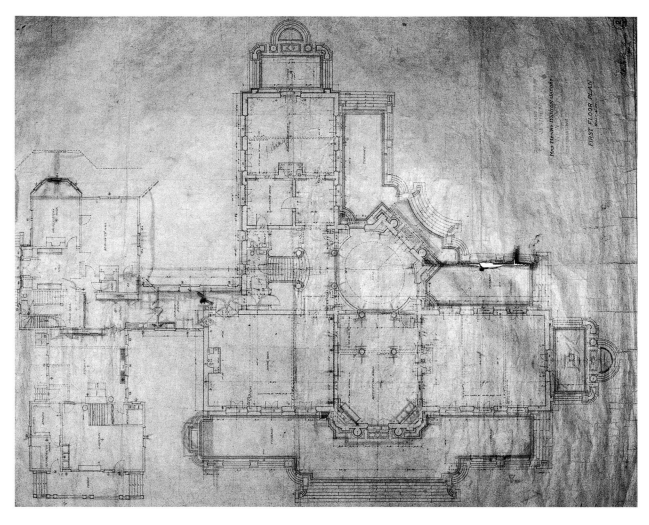

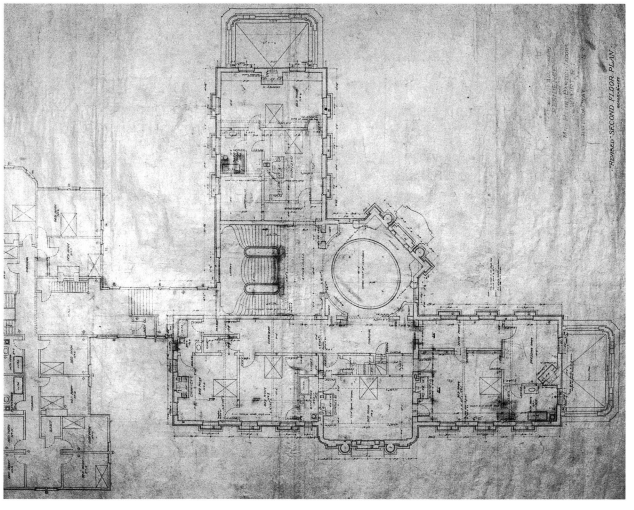

*Figs. 1-18, 1-19.
Drawings for
Dr. and Mrs. Henry
Barton Jacobs house,
Newport, Rhode
Island, 1901–03.*

skies and buildings whose stone facades seemed to project a luminous glow. However, Eggers was not merely a renderer. His main interest lay not in the production of drawings as such, but rather in the study and presentation of architectural designs. He always considered himself a designer, and the rendered drawing as just one stage in the process of designing a building. Nevertheless, Pope came to rely almost exclusively on Eggers's superior skills in the production of renderings.

Design Method

Pope's and Egger's design process was fully evolved by the time Eggers documented it in his article "The Genesis of a Rendering," in *Pencil Points* 3 (November 1922), where he used Pope's project for the Moses Taylor estate (1922–27) near Newport, Rhode Island, as an example. In an initial interview, the architect and client would discuss an appropriate style. In this case, Mrs. Taylor had expressed a definite preference for the French chateau style. The client and architect would jointly consult the standard works on the desired style, including Pope's stock of printed and photographic images as well as his own collection of large-format photographs taken during his sojourn as a *pensionnier* or later, while on vacations in Europe. These were often included in written specifications to indicate a particular desired effect. The choice of style was then checked against the site conditions to verify its appropriateness to local topography.

There were also other sources for precedents. Pope would often "recycle" a favorite design that had been rejected by a previous client or was unsuccessful in competition. He also frequently used the work of McKim as a basis for his own projects. Although this may have been simply out of respect for his mentor's design ability, it was probably more of an effort to demonstrate that he could improve on McKim's *parti* for a certain problem.

Once a stylistic decision had been made, the plan was determined in a process that developed progressively from rough freehand studies to ruled sketch plans, often on gridded paper (fig. 1-20). Next, rough elevations, primarily studies in mass, were sketched (fig. 1-21). To maintain a relationship with the site, a plot plan was drawn to locate the building. These studies were followed by a slightly and indefinitely drawn perspective that was proportionately scaled to the plan. The ultimate form of details was determined on the final rendering, which was used as both the basis for further design development and as a presentation piece for the client's approval (fig. 1-22). This would seem to follow the Beaux-Arts method, in which the plan is the initial and primary determinant of basic form. Eggers's and Pope's method seemed to differ with respect to the manner in which the shape

of individual elements was determined. These three-dimensional forms were determined primarily by their appearance on a rendering, a perspective drawing, a further indication that Pope and Eggers gave the drawing a certain primacy in their practice.

Once approved, the rendering and sketch plans would be used to develop final details and working drawings. A high degree of control over individual architectural and decorative pieces was maintained by executing large numbers of full-size drawings and plaster models of details, and in some cases, when the budget allowed, models of the entire building were made. In selecting details, Pope often consulted his own measured drawings from his days at the American Academy in Rome. As a result, certain favorite motifs frequently appear. A particular favorite was the Ionic order of the Theater of Marcellus. (Pope kept his own measured drawing of the building on a wall in his office.) However, in developing other details, Eggers and Pope would often consult—as was typical of any architect of the period—the standard sourcebooks on decorative details, such as books on English manor houses, and the works of Pugin, Stuart and Revett, Letarouilly, and d'Espouy.

In analyzing Pope's design process, one cannot help being surprised by the strongly pictorial approach he and Eggers pursued, according to which architectural elements were developed in relation to their effect in a drawing. In order for this method to succeed in three dimensions, it required the development of a rendering style with a high level of specificity of form that could convey an understanding of small details. It further demanded that the renderer be well acquainted with the specifics of formal precedents and understand what the building would actually look like when the designs were translated from two dimensions to three. The point of view employed in the drawings was necessarily one in which a minimum of distortion occurred. In other words, the drawings conveyed a certain photographic quality. This quality, or property, of Eggers's renderings may have been influenced by Pope's photographs and their explicit documentary nature. Certainly some of Eggers's highly detailed renderings were influenced by photographs of buildings. Those for the James Swan Frick house in suburban Baltimore, drawn some years after the house was completed, were clearly based on photographs.

The indefinite nature of the early design sketches implied that the specifics of architectural form could be changed and altered in consultation between Pope and Eggers, which allowed Pope to apportion his level of involvement with both the client and the design as he saw fit.

By delegating authority in a manner that emulated the *patron* of an atelier, Pope could act as critic on several projects simultaneously, and he would often callously apply a heavy grease pencil to Eggers's fine

*Figs. 1-20–1-22.
Glen Farm (Moses
Taylor house),
Newport, Rhode
Island, 1922–27.
Freehand sketch,
rough elevation, and
final rendering.*

renderings. When Pope was away from the office, he would design by telephone. After Pope became seriously ill in late 1935, Eggers and a trusted assistant would shuttle drawings from the office to Pope's house uptown, where Pope would mark them up. Then the often crestfallen pair would return to the office to execute the required corrections. But despite this apparent abuse, both Eggers and Pope produced better designs when they worked together. Pope's former employees regarded him with a mixture of deep respect for his ability and resentment for the brusque treatment they received. His attitude toward them appears to have been quite complicated. With some, he would abandon his businesslike front and chat about his career and early days with McKim and Ware in a nostalgic manner.

In a manner typical of the Beaux-Arts-trained architect, Pope established a personal hierarchy for the types of commission he sought. He disdained almost all commercial commissions, preferring monuments and large residences. This inclination coincides with the French academic tradition's preference for public buildings and palaces—buildings that Pope sought to translate into their American equivalents. Not surprisingly, Pope's oeuvre is dominated by large domestic and public commissions, while his few commercial ventures are not successful.

Pope seemed to have an almost reverential approach to historical architectural styles as points of departure for his designs. Accepting the stylistic eclecticism of McKim's generation, he approached historical styles as the basis for architectural exploration. He was primarily interested in producing an interpretation or synthetic version of a style generated from its underlying principles. In other words, he did not wish to create new styles, but rather to recreate or adapt existing ones to reflect American and classical precedent. This approach would seem to elucidate two aspects of his architectural persona. First, he held a conservative belief in the power and validity of classical form—no new and distinct style should be created. Second, this tenacious adherence to classicism may also have been an expression of insecurity, demonstrating that he lacked the confidence to go beyond style. However, Pope's contemporary William Adams Delano believed that Pope failed to live up to his artistic potential.

Whatever Pope's motivation, he quietly developed a distinctly and consciously American interpretation of classicism, in which American forms of the late eighteenth and early nineteenth century, as seen in such buildings as the Old Patent Office, The Old City Hall in Washington, D.C., and George Washington's Mount Vernon, were incorporated into his architectural vocabulary.

At the same time that Eggers joined Pope in 1909, Daniel P. Higgins (1886–1953) joined the firm, and he subsequently became Pope's other informal partner. It appears that Pope never entered into a formal partnership agreement with either Eggers or Higgins. Pope did, however, share profits and delegate some decision-making powers to both Eggers and Higgins, while retaining ultimate veto power. According to legend, Pope first noticed Higgins, an amateur boxer, at a match that provided the entertainment for a "smoker." Pope admired the pugnacious personality of Higgins and hired him as the firm's accountant. Attending night classes at New York University's School of Architecture, Higgins eventually received his degree, but his function in the office was definitely non-architectural. His gregarious personality made him a perfect salesman, and the ideal associate for a man whose professional manner was extremely reserved. A politically active Democrat and a strong supporter of the Roman Catholic Church, Higgins became the friend of Mayor La Guardia as well as members of the Roman Catholic hierarchy, associations that he used to obtain commissions for the office.

Family, Clients, and Colleagues

In 1912, Pope married Sadie Jones, the daughter of "robber baron" Pembroke Jones and later the stepdaughter of Henry Walters. Jones amassed his early wealth as a blockade runner during the Civil War and subsequently became a successful rice plantation owner and a majority stockholder in the Atlantic Coast Line railway. Sadie's mother later married Henry Walters, a Baltimore railroad magnate and art collector related to the Delano family, a connection that became useful much later when Franklin Delano Roosevelt became President of the United States.

Although impossible to prove definitively, it appears that Pope actively sought a rich wife. He often summered in Newport as the guest of his client Stuart Duncan as well as Pembroke Jones. He was about thirty-eight years old, already a successful architect, and had been listed in the *New York Social Register* since 1907. He was certainly a prime candidate for matrimony. Sadie was almost twenty years younger and had recently made her debut in Newport. The marriage would eliminate any financial worries on Pope's part, giving him the freedom to pursue prestigious projects that would aggrandize his status as an architect. His marriage seemed quite successful—he became a doting father to his two children, Mary and Jane—but also gave Pope the social stature that he lacked in comparison to such contemporaries as William Adams Delano, Chester Aldrich, or Thomas Hastings.

Pope's office attracted a very unusual group of employees in that they were all talented and ambitious college graduates, as opposed to unschooled apprentices, who stayed for a relatively short time before they set out for themselves in the fields of architecture and construction. In the 1930s, Pope could afford to be selective and paid a relatively low wage—thirty-five to forty-five dollars a week. Photographs of the drafting rooms seem typically spartan. Pope's personal offices were elegantly appointed, but not ostentatious. He kept an office at 1131 Broadway, near Madison Square, until 1907 when he moved to 527 Fifth Avenue, a few blocks above Forty-second Street. Although the office moved three times before the end of his career, it was always located at a prestigious address on Fifth Avenue in the vicinity of Forty-sixth Street.

With Eggers and Higgins as his assistants, Pope could afford to be absent from the firm for extended periods. He would customarily spend the month of August in Newport, refusing to return for any reason —even, as an apocryphal example, to present the design drawings for the Cloisters personally to John D. Rockefeller Jr., who, insulted, awarded the contract to Allen and Collins.

Pope's seeming aloofness to those who were not close friends was exacerbated after his daughter Mary's death in a car accident in 1930. Pope withdrew from all but the most important projects for several years, and his later illness would further aggravate this reclusive trait.

This progressive introversion was a continuous hindrance to the firm. Usually Pope would be quite involved with the clients in the early stages of design and then his interest in them would wane. He would subsequently assign more design responsibility to the chief designer (Eggers, Young, or Philip Will Jr.) or the supervising architect for the project. With particularly demanding clients, Pope would, absent himself from the design process after initial consultation. This often created a situation in which Eggers, who stammered nervously, would be forced to compel some junior draftsman to conduct business with a particularly cantankerous client. In time, Pope's relationship with his clients became formulaic. The prospective client would meet Pope, who would enthusiastically offer suggestions, but on subsequent meetings Pope would not be available.

Pope, however, continued to maintain a cordial relationship with the architectural press. He had a longstanding friendship with the New York *Tribune*'s art critic Royal Cortissoz, who began his career as a draftsman in McKim's office. Pope must have become acquainted with Cortissoz as a result of their mutual association with the American Academy in Rome, as Cortissoz was an early promoter of the Academy and of Pope's work. Cortissoz's specific definition of good architecture was that it must result from the study and adaptation of historical models.

Pope's attitude toward precedent coincided almost exactly with that of Cortissoz, who was always sympathetic to Pope's work.

Pope, not above self-promotion, agreed around 1924 to participate in the production of a monograph of his work. *The Architecture of John Russell Pope* was produced as a series of three large-format unbound folios, with adulatory introductions by Cortissoz accompanying each volume. Printed in installments, the last volume was not published until 1930. Due in part to a small print run, the book was not considered influential. Furthermore, by the time the last volume was published, the modernist style was well ensconced in America and interest in contemporary classically-inspired architecture was waning; the monograph does not appear to have been reviewed by any journal.

Despite having joined professional organizations at an early stage of his career, Pope, not surprisingly, was rarely an active participant in these societies. His apparent lack of support did not prevent him from being made a Fellow of the AIA in 1908. From the early 1920s onward, he received a variety of accolades. In 1922, he received the Medal of the Legion of Honor from the French government in recognition of his country house work. Yale University awarded him an honorary master's degree for his development of the first comprehensive scheme for the development of the university campus. In 1927, he was elected to the American Academy of Arts and Letters, succeeding John Singer Sargent. Columbia University followed Yale in 1929, awarding him a doctorate in letters for his contribution to the field of architecture. In 1933, the City College of New York bestowed the Townsend Harris Medal for distinguished alumni on him. He was a frequent participant in exhibitions at the Architectural League, but never assumed any personal responsibility within the club, leaving this obligation to the more affable Higgins. His involvement in the AIA was also minimal, with one isolated exception: he raised a large sum of money for the restoration of its headquarters building known as the Octagon. After this, Pope's further involvement in any professional organization was limited to the American Academy in Rome. He had a deep sense of allegiance and obligation to the organization, and from 1916 served on the jury for the Rome Prize in architecture. In 1925 he was elected as trustee of the American Academy and served as its president from 1933 to 1937.

CHAPTER 2

Commercial Buildings

The design of commercial buildings presented Pope with a contradiction. Their essentially utilitarian nature was at variance with his desire to create buildings characterized by an overwhelming, classically based formalism. Pope's belief in the ascendancy of a severe, grandiose image over functional concerns was clear from his few commercial designs, which he attempted to approach as yet another vehicle by which he could explore the nature of monumental classicism. His known commercial oeuvre is rather small and seems limited for the most part to prestigious commissions. It includes at least nine skyscraper designs (one built), two railway stations (one built), a suburban bank, a market (project), a Fifth Avenue shop, and a film studio (project). Of the fifteen projects, the designs must surely have struck his clients as too grand and expensive.

In considering these projects, one must question the clients' motivations in engaging Pope, who was indifferent to such commissions. The answer can only lie in the clients' desire for the buildings to carry a particular image, and their corresponding belief that Pope could best provide it. Businessmen wanted their offices viewed in the same light as town halls and monuments, and the classical tower came to signify the civic, philanthropic, or benevolent qualities of commercial enterprise.

SKYSCRAPERS

Pope's earliest dated skyscraper design was for Rector's Hotel (1909) in New York. Designed in an exceedingly exuberant Beaux-Arts manner, the fourteen-story mansard-roofed building included a large restaurant on the ground floor. The axis of its centrally placed entry bisects oval-shaped lobbies at the rear of the building. Interior elevations matched the exterior in their accretions of Louis XV decoration. At the same time, there was a studied rigidity in the building's organization that acted to defeat the flow of the rococo concoctions. Although the rococo was frequently favored for luxury hotels of this period, the style was atypical for Pope. He had produced

only three other designs in the "modern French" mode, all houses of several years earlier—the Stow (1903), Jacobs (1901–03), and Leeds (1907) houses. It is likely that Rector requested a building in that style, since Pope would surely have known that it was somewhat retardataire. Nevertheless, he presented extensive drawings. Pope's plan was rejected in favor of a more conservative design by D. H. Burnham and Co., which was, however, distinctly similar to Pope's. Burnham's effort may have been enhanced by copies of Pope's design, a fact which may have justified Pope's filing a copyright application—a rare act for an architect.

Pope's second high rise design, for a bank building in New York (c. 1915–19), is known through a single rendering (fig. 2-1) and a 1919 copyright application. In developing the design, which Pope did not identify, but which was probably the Redmond Bank, he followed the well-established division of the structure into a decorated base and crown with a relatively plain shaft. The cubic base is articulated by a double-height, slightly projecting Tuscan colonnade. Two overwhelmingly ponderous wings terminate the ground floor composition. Oversized window openings, surmounted by bas-relief panels, further articulate the mass. A Doric frieze runs around this lower part of the building and is topped by a parapet, which is in turn articulated as a hypaethral space. The centrally located tower, whose major decoration consists of quoined corner returns, rises from a setback at the cornice line of the adjacent buildings. A thermal window marks the point of juncture between base and tower. A double-height colonnade completes the shaft and signals the base of the building's terminal element. The crown is articulated as a set-back, steep-hipped mansard roof with *oeil-de-boeuf* dormers.

There is very little new or even up-to-date in this scheme, and one can discern at the street elevation an effort to monumentalize the building through the use of overscale classical elements borrowed from a combination of well-known precedents and other early works by Pope. The base is closely linked to Pope's own plans for low-rise structures such as the

*Fig. 2-1. Redmond
Bank (unbuilt),
New York, c. 1915–19.*

Fig. 2-2. Massachusetts Bonding Insurance Company (unbuilt), New York, c. 1920.

Fig. 2-3. Undated scheme, probably for a bank building.

Macdonough Memorial in Plattsburgh, New York (1914–26), the Richmond Terminal (1913–19), and the Lincoln Birthplace Museum (1908). The upper levels and termination are typical of New York skyscraper designs of the period. However, Pope virtually ignored the shaft of the building, which, with the exception of the quoined returns, was undecorated. Its disquieting proportions demonstrate Pope's inability to integrate a vertical element into his classical schema. In the terminus there were vague references to the Mausoleum at Halicarnassus, a source that Pope consulted in his roughly contemporary Temple of the Scottish Rite in Washington, D.C. (1910–17).

Over the next few years, Pope continued to refine the design, apparently reflecting the changes in New York zoning law, but the modifications to the exterior scheme still could not reconcile the incompatibility of the essentially horizontal classical mode with the verticality of the skyscraper. The proposed banking floor demonstrates Pope's continued reliance on precedent insofar as it is a copy of his own Rome Prize design.

However, despite the apparent problems he had with the project, Pope was beginning to create his own formal, monumental image for the American skyscraper. In its failure to synthesize the individual elements into an integrated image, this project vividly demonstrates Pope's manner of composing using a classical "kit of parts."

A third project, for the Massachusetts Bonding Insurance Company (c. 1920), was for the renovation of a skyscraper (fig. 2-2), a work in which Pope's objective appears to have been the creation of a monumental entry to a rather ordinary loft building. A pair of Doric columns *in antis* flank the entrance, while a denticulated frieze bears the name of the company. This frieze is topped by a pair of *clathri*—panels enclosing iron security bars—flanking a central cartouche containing a clock. The formal severity of this doorway stands in direct contrast to the building, and is set off from the mass of the structure by a large reveal joint. The lighter shading of this portion of the building in the rendering further emphasizes and accentuates the incongruity of the relationship between the entry and the rest of the building.

An undated scheme, probably of the 1920s, for a bank building further illustrates Pope's inability to create a classically monumental skyscraper (fig. 2-3). In his rapid sketch, a six-story shaft negates the vertical thrust of a classically decorated ground floor. Atop this bland shaft the vertical motion is further

impeded by a frieze and cornice. Above, the building steps pyramidally, each corner articulated by torchères. This pyramidal form is surmounted by a terminus based on the outline of the Mausoleum at Halicarnassus. The building lacks any sense of composition and balance.

Not long after the publication of Hugh Ferriss's skyscraper envelope studies in the *New York Times Magazine*, Pope produced his most successful high rise design. The project for the Harriman National Bank (1924) was almost visionary (fig. 2-4). The forty-story building project had lain fallow for several years, until Pope, in his almost customary manner, resurrected the design and offered it to real estate developer August Heckscher. In his search for an appropriate precedent, Pope had finally struck upon a shape that would both convey the image of monumental severity and accommodate the essential verticality of the skyscraper. He had reduced the skyscraper to an elemental, geometricized, classical mass: the obelisk. The tapered volume provided an articulation of verticality that required no further decoration. As a freestanding tower, the building was also, by coincidence of form, a very modern skyscraper in the manner of Raymond Hood's emphatically vertical American Radiator Building (1924) in

New York. For this project, Pope had succeeded in producing a building of imposing monumentality and rigid dignity that rivaled the images of Hugh Ferriss in their expression of force and power. In its clarity of form, it also rivals contemporary designs such as Bertram Goodhue's Convocation Tower project for New York (1921) and the Los Angeles Municipal Tower (1927) by Parkinson, Austin, and Martin. That the building was never built demonstrates Pope's unwillingness to rescale the project to fit the client's needs and further indicates his lack of interest in carrying a commercial building to fruition.

In subsequent projects of the 1920s, Pope retreated from the elegantly severe Harriman/Heckscher project to pursue more decorative solutions. His 1927 study for a bank and office building at Wall Street and Broadway demonstrates his continued failure in this search (fig. 2-5). Again, as in the Harriman/Heckscher scheme, a tapered central mass buttressed by ornamented setbacks at the corners reinforced the monolithic image. Once more, the building is terminated by a stylized interpretation of the Mausoleum at Halicarnassus, which in turn is surmounted by a large globe. While the stripped classicism of the upper levels is in keeping with the general reductionist spirit of Pope's work, the lower, banking level is more

blatantly classical; the transition between the two is achieved by means of a stringcourse with frieze band windows. Yet despite references to well-known sources, the parti fails as a skyscraper base because the excessive detail makes it seem incapable of supporting the awkward mass above.

Two years later, in a study for an office building, Pope attempted to resolve many of the problems apparent in the previous design. The termination of the building, based again on the Mausoleum at Halicarnassus, was reduced to a more coherent shape with fewer details. The monolithic impression of the supporting shaft was maintained through the use of setback buttressing at the building's corners. These buttresses acted as a foil to the corner returns of the building's terminus. The sense of verticality was reinforced by projecting window reveals. Again, the building's weakest point was its base, whose superfluity of decoration, large openings, and pilaster-on-pilaster decorated interstices seem disproportionate to the solidity and mass above.

Pope's one realized skyscraper, built in 1929 for Cincinnati Gas and Electric (fig. 2-6) embodies the principles of design that Pope had been developing over the previous decade. In basic form, a centrally placed monolithic shaft rises from a ground floor dec-

orated with the Doric order. It is terminated by a stylized interpretation of, again, the Mausoleum at Halicarnassus. Setbacks at the base of the shaft and upper terminations are decorated with classical torchères.

In previous projects, Pope's ground floor solutions lacked sufficient force and severity to produce an adequate image of building support. In this building, however, the use of a strong Doric colonnade flanked by large corner portals provides a solid image of support. The intervening pilasters on the secondary side of the building, coupled with dark metal window sashes, further the image of a solid base. Here, Pope successfully integrated the severity and dignity of the obelisk design into his decorative formula.

In his last two skyscraper projects, Pope continued to experiment with the basic parti developed during the previous decade. In a 1932 proposal for a skyscraper at Park Avenue and Thirty-ninth Street (fig. 2-7), the problematic ground terminus of Pope's skyscrapers of the 1920s is more elegantly resolved by carrying the bulk of the building down to the ground floor and maintaining the motif of verticality through the use of accentuated shafts between the windows. Decorative elements are reduced to a minimum, eliminating any visual disparity between the base and shaft of the building. At

Fig. 2-8. Proposal for a skyscraper (unbuilt), New York, 1935.

a large severe Tuscan portico flanked by pavilions decorated with Tuscan pilasters and small doorways, announced the white entrance. Abutting the central unit, the two wings were simply articulated through the use of extremely large rectangular window openings. A large attic suggestive of a triumphal arch surmounted the composition and was meant to bear a sculptural program related to the theme of railroad travel.

The dominant portico, with its heavy column bases and sparsely decorated attic clearly resembled the entrance porticoes of New York's Pennsylvania Station. This and other McKim, Mead & White designs surely influenced Pope's project, and it is not surprising that he would have emulated his mentor's work: originality notwithstanding, replication of McKim's design would have proven that Pope was capable of producing designs of a quality equal to that of his advisor. Furthermore, the successful design of Pennsylvania Station spawned copies throughout the country, as the simple geometry and Roman classicism were easy models to emulate.

Pope's design derived its forceful impression from its massive scale and simplicity of form, which made excessive detail superfluous and inconsequential. However, despite the local newspaper critics' approval of the design, the station was not built due to the city's continued resistance to the proposed site.

In his next railroad station competition, for Jacksonville, Florida (1916), Pope presented a weak, poorly integrated scheme (fig. 2-11). But despite this, he did introduce a strong new element into his design: a centrally placed dome supported by a high double drum. The lower drum was articulated as a Greek cross with open bed pediments pierced by modified thermal windows, while the upper drum was an unadorned ring of masonry. Again, Pope appeared to be using McKim's architectural vocabulary in an attempt to do him one better. The somewhat unusual drum form may have been borrowed from the design of the National Museum of Natural History (1909) or McKim's Army War College in Washington, D.C. (1907). It also can be found in several reconstructions of the Roman baths of Caracalla and Diocletian as well as the Basilica of Constantine. At any rate, Pope had found a new application for McKim's forms. But whatever Pope's intentions in experimenting with the form, it was fortunate for him that the critics did not see the awkwardness of the design. Critical assessment of the domed railway station would have to wait.

In late 1916, the railway companies revived the Richmond project. As a result of the Jacksonville competition, Pope felt compelled to develop a new design for Richmond. In the new submission, Pope incorporated a dome over the central waiting room (fig. 2-13). The building as designed provided a strong and stable silhouette that relied heavily on its

Fig. 2-11. Jacksonville Terminal competition entry (unbuilt), Jacksonville, Florida, 1916.

Fig. 2-12. Revised proposal for Union Station, Richmond, Virginia, 1916 (completed 1919).

Fig. 2-13. Union Station, Richmond, Virginia, 1919.

Fig. 2-14. Union Station. Plan.

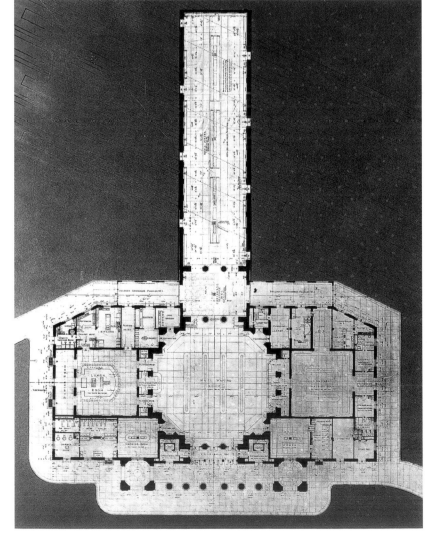

mass and proportions for its final effect. This composition dating from 1916, with the exception of steps leading up to the entrance, was intact when the building was completed in January 1919 (fig. 2-14). Pope's dome loomed over the surrounding streetscape, greatly enhancing the building's monumentality. This grandiloquent formal gesture provided Richmond with a solemn and triumphal gateway to a city that was still fondly referred to as the Capital of the Confederacy. Complete with imbrication, the dome was clearly based on McKim's Low Library at Columbia University (1893); however the Pantheon was, of course, the ultimate progenitor of this feature of the design.

Aside from the addition of a dome, other small changes were made to the facade. The openings in the corner pavilions became arches with large carved keystones. At the next level, large relief-flanked windows were added above the arches. The bases of the columns of the central portico were reduced in height. The entrance was clearly based on two Renaissance sources: Peruzzi's entrance to the Palazzo Massimo alle Colonne and Giuliano da Sangallo's porch at the Villa Medici at Poggio a Caiano, sources Pope should have known firsthand from his travels in Italy. The colonnade was topped by a parapet bearing inscriptions and flanking a centrally placed clock supported by allegorical figures of Progress and Industry.

The interior plan was changed from the first proposal (fig. 2-14). The necessary services now radiated from the white waiting room. The rest of the plan was simplified into large, clearly defined elements whose volume was expressed externally as separate masses. The entrance to the station was the most awkward element of the design because Pope chose to change orders on the interior of the building from Tuscan to Ionic. To avoid the problem of conflicting proportions and to reduce congestion at the entrance, he simply omitted the order, leaving a large opening spanned by a stone lintel with no visible support (figs. 2-15, 2-16).

The entry led into the large, domed waiting room where gray Tennessee marble wainscotting was topped by gray Indiana limestone. Paired Ionic columns based on those of the Theater of Marcellus in Rome framed access to the concourse to the north, while Ionic pilasters based on the same source framed the ticket area and the dining areas to the east and west (fig. 2-17). Above, a strong denticulated cornice defined the springing of the dome. Beneath it, a sphere eight feet in diameter hung in the center of the waiting room, just as a globe was suspended from the top of McKim's dome in Low Library.

In the western wing of the building the interior was decorated with roundels and blind arcading. A central skylight provided illumination for a lunch counter that was separated from the rest of the diners by a colonial-revival-style glass and cast-iron screen.

The ticket counter at the east side of the white waiting room connected to the black service area that was entered from a separate entrance to the east. A small hallway led from the black waiting room to the Ionic-pilastered train concourse. Passengers descended from this long hall to the trains below.

The Richmond station represented another step in Pope's successful development of a formal vocabulary that would continue to be refined and reiterated in later projects. Each step was characterized by a tendency toward classicized geometric simplicity in massing and a corresponding austerity in plan and elevation. In this design, Pope composed an integrated unity out of this distinct vocabulary. Whether or not he debased or violated the canon of associations in his use of the dome, Pope's application of the form further explicates his approach to classical sources. Any monumental form was appropriate for any building type if it succeeded in achieving the proper effect.

SMALLER COMMISSIONS

With the exception of his New York City Market (1918), the small commercial commissions in Pope's office have been ascribed by former employees to Otto Eggers. Nevertheless, they were produced under Pope's supervision, and even if he expressed a certain disinterest in such work, it should be considered a part of his oeuvre. The earliest of these, the proposed New York City Market, appears to have been connected with an attempt to develop community markets throughout the city following the food riots that flared up during World War I. For this project, Pope developed an arcaded scheme that turned for its inspiration to the work of Brunelleschi and his Tuscan contemporaries. It closely resembled the Mercato Nuovo in Florence, a source well known to Beaux-Arts-trained architects, and thus it adds force to the theory that Pope intended to endow even the most mundane activities with a certain dignity by housing them in severe, monumental spaces. In this instance, the only relief from austerity was achieved through the use of mannerist cartouches on the second level. The visual effect of the exterior was extremely successful, and the groin-vaulted interior provided a lavish setting for a simple market.

As a type, the small bank building was better suited to Pope's particular brand of classicism. The First National Bank of Mamaroneck, New York (1929, now drastically altered), built in Eggers's hometown, was an excellent adaptation of the Georgian town house form. The building possessed a clarity and strength of form that was reminiscent of the buildings of James Stuart on St. James's Square in London, which Pope most likely would have seen on his many trips to England.

Fig. 2-15

42 COMMERCIAL BUILDINGS

*Fig. 2-15. Union
Station. Entrance
portico.*

*Fig. 2-16. Union
Station. Entrance.*

*Fig. 2-17. Union
Station. Main
concourse.*

Fig. 2-16

Fig. 2-17

CHAPTER 3

RESIDENTIAL ARCHITECTURE

Fig. 3-1. Final scheme for Dr. and Mrs. Henry Barton Jacobs house, Newport, Rhode Island, 1901–03.

John Russell Pope's earliest work was primarily domestic and coincided chronologically with work he performed in Price's office. Following what one would assume was the normal progression for an architect of the period, Pope began by designing small summer houses for lesser-known clients, advanced to small outbuildings and renovations of summer houses for the socially prominent, and eventually became the architect of large country estates. Although his interest in residential work waned after 1930, during his thirty-four years of independent practice, Pope created some of the finest American house designs of the period.

While Pope's stylistic development generally followed the vogue of nationally popular styles, his singular talent was to penetrate beyond mere copyist approaches to probe the underlying principles and sources to produce forceful restatements of a particular style. This mastery imbued his designs with an authenticity that was lacking in the work of colleagues such as Delano & Aldrich, Charles Platt, or Henry Hornbostel. Pope's ability to distill styles to their essences and the severity of his adaptations evoked a dignity that especially appealed to the conservative tastes of his wealthy clients.

By the time Pope came of age professionally at the turn of the century, lavish town and country houses had come a long way from the Andalusias and the Lyndhursts of the pre-Civil War period. Richard Morris Hunt and McKim, Mead & White had blazed the trail with a succession of extravagant town and country houses in traditional European idioms, testifying that the course of empire and wealth had decisively moved across the Atlantic with no apparent loss; as it had been in Europe, so it would be in America. No styles associated with previous periods of wealth and power were missing in the repertoire of forms these architects employed, which were spread from New England to the colonialized South.

As Pope began his career, the American country house as a type was already well defined. During the 1870s, Americans escaping summer in the city began to expect something more substantial than the artificial life of great hotels and villas in the springs, shore, or resort towns, and thus began to build more permanent places. In the 1880s and 1890s, Stanford White, Charles Follen McKim, and Richard Morris Hunt set the pace with such famous houses as Biltmore, Ochre Point, Florham, and Ochre Court. By 1900, the country house phenomenon was well established, with magazines such as *Country Life in America* promoting the accompanying lifestyle.

At the same time, there seemed to be a reaction to such examples of conspicuous consumption. In creating her own house, The Mount (1902), in Lenox, Massachusetts, Edith Wharton essentially essayed an alternative. Her smaller, less presumptuous, and perhaps more urbane approach to the design of the country estate became the most popular type of rural residence by the 1920s. Her reaction to the excesses of the previous generation, in keeping with Herbert Croly's exhortations of architectural restraint in his journal *Architectural Record*, set the tone for country house design as Pope entered the field. That most of Pope's earliest residential commissions were for country houses reflects the clients' greater willingness to experiment with a building that was neither used year-round nor constantly in the public eye. Nevertheless, his houses were designed as public statements, confronting not the relatively simple problem of habitation, but rather that of architectural representation. His clients, mostly conservative in taste and politics, expected their houses to project a particularly reserved image of power. Pope's earliest contributions can be seen as an attempt to further define the reserved image of the country house type developed by Price and McKim, in which the power of basic form was emphasized over decoration.

Pope produced a great number of town and country houses in modern French, Tudor, American Georgian, English Georgian, Adamesque, and Louis XVI styles. Although there was significant chronological overlap, these may be grouped into five stages falling between the years 1900 to 1937.

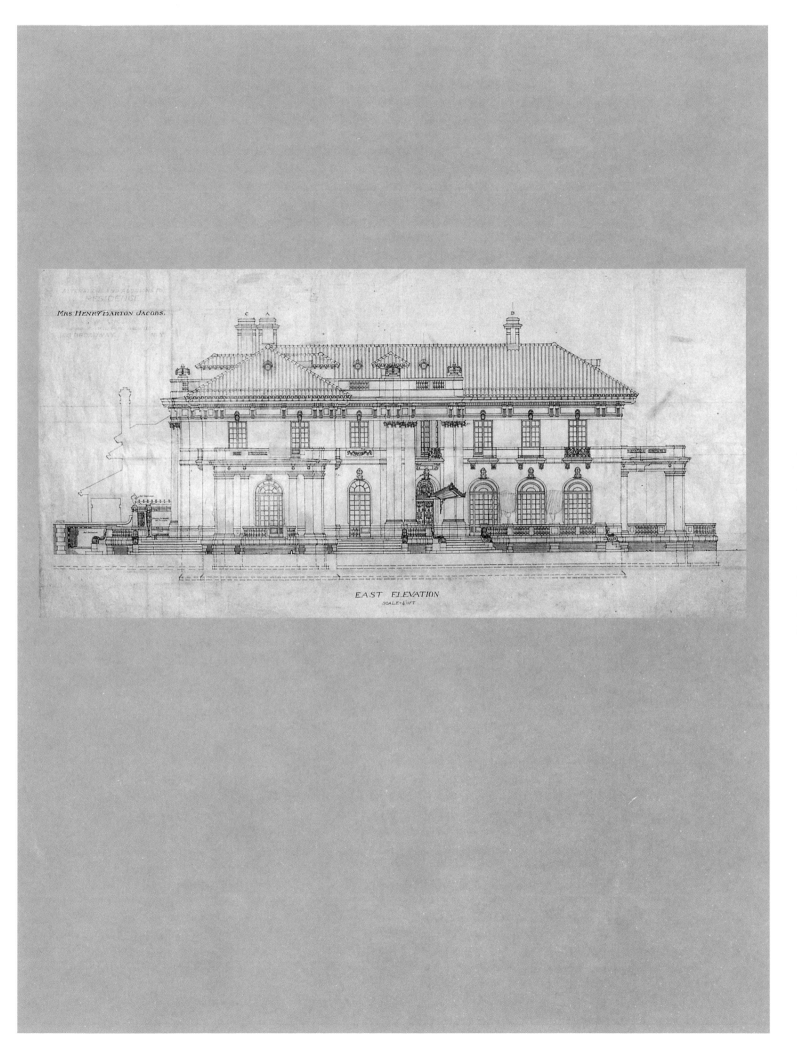

ALTERATION AND ADDITIONS TO
RESIDENCE

MRS. HENRY BARTON JACOBS.

EAST ELEVATION
SCALE-¼-FT

1900–1907:
ANXIETY OF INFLUENCE

Pope's two earliest commissions, the Jacobs (1901–03) and Stow (1903) houses, both large country estates for minor socialites, were begun as independent commissions while he was still working in Price's office. They immediately attracted critical attention and tentative approval for his treatment of classical form and building volumes. Critic Barr Ferree's later inclusion of Pope's Stow house in his *Country Estates and Gardens* (1906) signaled the architect's arrival as an important residential designer: Ferree discussed Pope's work with the same interest as he did that of his mentors.

While over time Pope shifted his exploration of architectural paradigms from European to more American sources, his earliest work explored the modern French style, which was not surprising given the then current interest in European artistic developments, general feelings of cultural inferiority on the part of Americans, and Pope's recent return from France. These designs reflected the bold expressiveness of the modern French, but Pope adapted the style to the more severe climate and conservative sensibility of his New England clients, creating through a consequent reduction of exterior ornament an imposing and serious image appropriate to the taste of the wealthy American.

The patronage history of Pope's first major independent domestic commission, the Newport, Rhode Island, summer house for Dr. and Mrs. Henry Barton Jacobs of Baltimore, is unclear. The commission may have come from Bruce Price, who was well connected in Baltimore. Or Jacobs may have known Pope's uncle, Dr. Alfred Loomis, from their association with Harvard. Or since Pope referred to his clients in letters as "Uncle Jake" and "Aunt Mary," Jacobs may have been some distant relation. Mary Frick Garrett Jacobs, heiress to part of the Baltimore & Ohio Railroad fortune, had summered in Newport, and in 1899 purchased the Hitchcock-Travers house, designed by Richard Morris Hunt. The house, which had been completed in 1872, was outmoded, and required extensive remodeling or renovation.

The Jacobses apparently first approached Pope in 1901 and by early 1902 the final scheme had been produced (fig. 3-1). Instead of using drawings to describe the style of the various rooms, Pope scrawled the style of the room in pencil on the drawing. This could indicate either that he had little interest in interior design, or, since this was a summer house, that he preferred a more ad hoc approach. It could also mean that the surviving drawings date from a period too early for detailed interior drawings.

The exterior of the house was generally treated in the same manner as the slightly later Stow house. The main and garden entrances are flanked by engaged Ionic columns, but on the garden facade simple arched windows replace the arcade. The resultant stark wall was softened by vines trained into a *guilloche* pattern. As was to be expected in Newport, "the Trouville of America," the Jacobs house was decidedly more flamboyant than the later Stow house on less fashionable Long Island. The exterior details were French-inspired in contrast to the Italianate massing of the building. Built to subsume the existing Richard Morris Hunt house, its L-shaped plan was necessitated by the tight Newport site, the need for a screen to cover the older house, and a desire to produce a sense of visual space around the house.

The interior had an elliptical entry hall and the staircase was pure Beaux-Arts-inspired modern French. Predictably for a summer house, the major rooms were planned to open onto the south terraces overlooking the garden. The interiors were designed in an overelaborated rococo revival style that was marred only by a lapse into Georgian revival in the dining room. The gilt furniture and rose-colored hangings were all designed or selected by Pope.

A key element of this project was the design of the parterre and approach to the house. Half of the grounds were left to pasture, creating upon entry a controlled panoramic view of the estate, while large shade trees were replanted to soften the severity of the main entrance. The lush south-facing garden, with cruciform parterres and ponds that swept down from the main body of the building, effected a stark contrast to the austere planarity of the southern wall, whose only relief was achieved with trained ivy swags and balconettes.

In overall appearance, the house owes much to Pope's French training. Aside from the exterior decoration, it was an up-to-date rendition of a villa in the modern French mode. The fanciful plan forms in the main hall and stairway as well as the landscaping made this building Pope's most literal essay in the Beaux-Arts style. To his credit, one already can see in this early work the emergence of certain characteristics of his later approach to architectural styles. This is most clear in his attempt to maintain a certain sobriety while working in an exuberant style by applying decoration sparingly to the exterior, a design characteristic that would later win him much praise.

The Jacobs house was generally viewed as a critical success. It was noted for its playful and picturesque manipulation of the French style, as well as for its sober and dignified character. In the March 1908 issue of *The Architectural Review*, however,

Stuart Bartlett derisively described the house as a kind of "fairy architecture of some sort any one may recognize . . . . No one can escape the sphere of pretension, of bombast, almost joyous devil-may-care impertinence that the house exudes."

The W. L. Stow house in Roslyn, New York, completed in the fall of 1903 (destroyed, fig. 3-2), rested on a slight rise commanding the Long Island countryside. As with the Jacobs house, little is known of the patronage history of this commission. Although decidedly French-influenced in decorative treatment, the house gave an overall impression more reminiscent of an Italian Renaissance villa. Its H-plan was distinguished by an arcaded garden front and a triumphal-arched entry whose noble and sober outward appearance was created by the relative restraint of the exterior decoration. The dramatically molded keystones and balconettes contrasted with a flat concrete wall surface that was broken only by a proportionally correct frieze, which in turn united the three sections of the house. The frieze did not, however, mitigate the painfully incoherent relationship between the vast wall space and the excessively ornate decorative elements.

The plan and its clarity demonstrate the influence of Bruce Price on Pope's work. As was typical of houses planned by his employer, the major rooms were grouped around a central entry hall, while eleven bedrooms and nine bathrooms were simply aligned on the second floor. In direct opposition to the clarity of the plan, each major room was decorated in a different historical style: François 1er for the hall, a Spanish Renaissance salon, a Tudor library, and an Italian Renaissance dining room (fig. 3-3). This eclecticism was entirely accepted during the period, for it reflected the reigning belief that America was heir to the entire artistic legacy of the Old World.

The gardens designed by Pope for the Stow house consisted of a series of terraces with rusticated walls whose architectonic forcefulness overpowered the plantings even when they matured. The landscaping did, however, accentuate the small rise and created a forceful image for the landscape setting, which held its own against the house. Contemporary critics were generally laudatory.

Another early commission, the renovation of newspaper publisher John Roll McLean's country house (completed 1903, later destroyed) on the western outskirts of Washington, D.C., continued the Georgian revival trend that Pope had begun in his almost contemporaneous work on the Perrin and Howard houses for Bruce Price. In this project for the owner of the *Washington Post* and the *Cincinnati Enquirer*, Pope's sparse treatment of architectural volumes worked to greater advantage in large part because the Georgian style was more conducive to such reductionist treatment. In fact, his choice of

this style was also a reflection of the social changes taking place at the time in Washington, D.C., and its suburbs.

In 1890, the nation's capital was not much more than a red brick Southern town. But after the World's Columbian Exposition of 1893 and the McMillan plan of 1901, the character of Washington changed rapidly. An incredible building spree began, creating vast residences along both Massachusetts Avenue and Sixteenth Street. Over the next few years, which corresponded with Pope's first years on his own, Washington was suddenly overrun with the moneyed and powerful from other parts of the country who realized the city now had a hand in controlling America's riches. The city underwent a sudden bonanza in house building and developed into a winter watering hole for high society, rivaling New York in its opulence.

Pope's work for Price on the Perrin (1902) and Howard (1907) houses must have been recognized, and his association with McKim certainly must have provided him with an entrée into the upper levels of Washington society. His appeal seems to have been limited to one section of the capital's elite: with the exception of another McLean commission (1907), all of his early houses were commissioned by members of the diplomatic corps or persons associated with the Foreign Affairs Committees on Capitol Hill. His skill in planning houses that functioned well for entertainment was appreciated by clients who had extensive social commitments. Pope was also able to provide such clients with appropriately understated expressions of wealth—images of quiet but never absent power, since for them the representation of power was the primary reason for building.

In the case of the McLean house, Pope's addition of a planar pilastered arcade served to reface, unify, and enlarge an older building. The house, with its new facade and rear addition, and despite Pope's awkward treatment of existing dormers, created a resolute image that was softened only by an extensive garden. Its plain, forceful image stimulated other residential commissions for Pope.

Whatever their critical acceptance, the Perrin, Howard, and McLean houses must be taken together as a developmental stage in Pope's search for the appropriately expressive residential form for a society whose relation to the arts has been frequently described as materialistic, self-conscious, insecure, and conservative. Although grandiose, each house plan had a clear and direct logic that was not obscured by excessive numbers of rooms or convoluted geometries. In these houses, Pope achieved the appearance of grandiosity and ostentation by the careful proportioning of their masses. In his adaptation of the modern French style, Pope melded visual images that he had experienced firsthand: Italian massing with French detail. This synthetic move created the

Fig. 3-2. W. L. Stow house, Roslyn, New York, 1903.

Fig. 3-3. Stow house. "Gold" room.

*Fig. 3-5. Middleton
Burrill house, Jericho,
New York, 1906.*

for the conservatory (fig. 3-8), an essential element for a building with no private outdoor spaces. Located above the stables, the concept for its interior peristyles would continue to be refined in Pope's various public and private works. Although the decorative elements of the house obscured the sense of proportion of the individual rooms, the relation between the width and depth was conveyed by skylights. With the exception of the highly ornate baroque salon, the relatively subdued interior design of the house was overwhelmed by Elsie de Wolfe's decorative efforts.

Although it is difficult to ascribe the design to a particular style, the overall effect captured the essence of a northern Italian Renaissance palazzo, though certain individual elements seem to have other Renaissance sources, such as the courtyard fountain, the voussoirs of the entry, the torus moulding, and the battered basement. Pope achieved a coherent Italianate effect by using massing, detail, and materials in a manner sympathetic to the Italianate style. By analytically distilling the essential components of the style, he then re-created it without descending into academic copying. At the same time, the house was designed in definite reaction to recent domestic architecture in Washington, which was much showier and more pretentious.

In the house for banker W. Storrs Wells (1907) at 16 East Fifty-seventh Street in New York, Pope was faced with an inherent contradiction in relation to the chosen style. The rococo interior implicitly demanded elaborate detail, yet the small size of the rooms suggested a restrained treatment that would not overpower the viewer. By limiting and flattening the ornament, as well as relying on monochromatic reliefs, Pope succeeded in producing a rococo scheme that respected the spatial integrity of the rooms. He adjusted the compression of ornament so that the decoration merely softened the room's volume rather than dominating it—a technique that would become a trademark of his design work. In this project one sees that Pope could not only adapt a European style to meet distinctly American needs, but also that he appears to have been able to calibrate the exuberance of a style to fit the needs of the particular client.

Up to this point, Pope's career seems to have gotten off to a slow and uneven start. It was during these first eight years of his practice that he developed the beginnings of a distinctive and exciting approach to form, decoration, and massing, an approach he applied with some facility to a number of styles. By no means had he reached a mature approach to design, but he had achieved some success in producing minor architectural gems, and probably just as importantly, had no major failures

Fig. 3-6

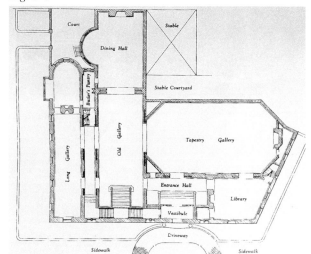

Fig. 3-7

Fig. 3-6. John Roll McLean house, Washington, D.C., 1907.

Fig. 3-7. McLean house. Plan.

Fig. 3-8. McLean house. Conservatory.

Fig. 3-8

53

to his discredit. By 1907, he was certainly considered a promising heir to the mantle of McKim as one of the best residential architects in the country.

1907–12: EARLY MATURITY

Around 1907, Pope's work became more carefully analytical, sober, and refined, poised somewhere between the banal or overly cautious and the grand image of restrained monumentality. He continued to adopt a severe and restrained approach to architectural styles, always emphasizing the supremacy of essential classical form over ornament. The country house commissions—in particular, two Long Island estates, Arlough (1907, destroyed, rebuilt 1910) in Westbury, designed for banker and diplomat Robert Low Bacon, and Chateauiver, the house for Commodore Charles A. Gould (1908, destroyed in 1954)—demonstrate Pope's continued experimentation with the reduction of architectural styles to their sheer essences.

Arlough demonstrates Pope's understanding of a style and his ability to develop it into a form at once familiar and personal. The house (fig. 3-9) was clearly derived from a polyglot of English and American sources, and was essentially an enlarged and stripped-down version of a colonial house. Since no clear plan has ever been published, further analysis of the importance of the house has been impeded.

In 1908, Pope renewed his professional association with the Gould family, designing a large country house for their thousand-acre estate in Greenlawn. With Chateauiver, one sees Pope reducing a style to its formal and material essences. Sketches for the building were made in September 1908, and construction began soon thereafter. With Gould's hunting interests in mind, the initial sketches were very academic adaptations of the Louis XII hunting box form, with the addition of rococo-inspired arcades at the ground-floor level. The overall effect of solidity and forcefulness was quite impressive. Based also on such small Louis XII hunting boxes as Les Grotteaux (1620) at Husseau sur Cosson, a small estate on the Cosson River in the Loire Valley between Chambord and Blois, the house acquired a Louis XVI–style addition in the form of the flat-roofed end pavilions. Even materials, such as Caen stone and yellow tinted stucco, were used to convey the image of France. The exuberant roofline of the central pavilion (fig. 3-10,) did not preclude the use of level cornices and simple details that Pope turned to their best advantage. While the extreme severity of the design, with its drastic economy of detail, produced an almost scaleless and impersonal appearance, a pleasing tension was created by the juxtaposition of the Louis XII and Louis XVI styles for the wings and the central pavilion. The shift in style suggests a change in taste over time, and may have been meant to give the house an aura of age.

In plan (fig. 3-11), the roughly H-shaped symmetry runs counter to the flamboyant roof. In typical fashion, a large hall mediated between the major public spaces of the houses, the main entrance, and the grand stairs leading to the bedrooms of the upper floors. The few surviving views of the interior

Fig. 3-9. Arlough (Robert Low Bacon house), Westbury, New York, 1907 (destroyed, rebuilt 1910).

Fig. 3-10. Chateauiver (Charles A. Gould house), Greenlawn, New York, 1908.

Fig. 3-11. Chateauiver. Plan.

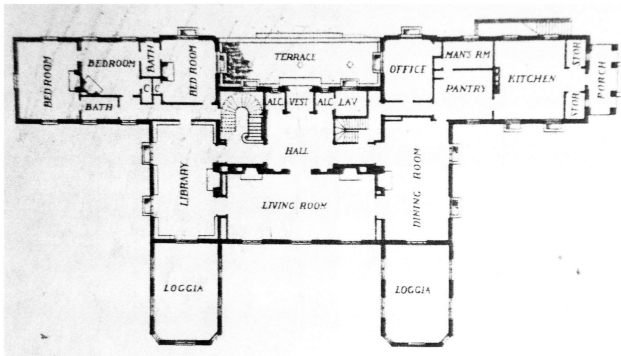

indicate, in contrast to the exterior appearance of the house, an opulent period treatment in the furnishings. It appears that the architectural tone of the library and dining room was set by Ionic pilasters with swagged and gilded capitals, typical features of French architecture of the eighteenth century, while the living room was much more sparsely decorated with simply paneled walls and doors.

The Bacon and Gould houses clearly demonstrate something new in American architecture: a more disciplined approach to historical precedents. Obviously not archaeologically correct, they nonetheless demonstrated a new rigor, a reaction to the eclectic and excessive application of detail in the work of Pope's contemporaries. With these houses, there is a further development in terms of the clarity of order evinced in their planning, a trait that would become a distinctive characteristic of Pope's later work.

In Pope's work thus far, we have seen him begin to distill a building's form and style and refine the architectural elements of massing, decoration, and planning to their essences. With the Hitt house (1907–09, demolished in 1970) in Washington, D.C., Pope realized the potential of this distillation process

With the Hitt house, Pope set a new standard for residential design in Washington by bringing this cosmopolitan European arrangement to an American house. He had finally created a domestic form that was formal, simple, and learned, rather than stiff, plain, and dry. The importance of the Hitt house in Pope's career cannot be overstated. The overwhelming propriety of the solution and its sober beauty seemed to epitomize the aspirations of American taste. Grand house design in Washington turned to a spare severity that emulated Pope's Hitt design, and with the completion of this house, Pope became one of the premier residential designers in America.

Pope's next major domestic commission in Washington, the Henry White house (1910–12) (fig. 5-15), was another great success and solidified his reputation. White had purchased a large lot on Sixteenth Street atop Meridian Hill, overlooking the city. It is not clear why White selected Pope, but the architect's previous association with McKim and the American Academy, his recent participation in the Lincoln Memorial competition, and his winning the Temple of the Scottish Rite competition certainly influenced White, and the success of Pope's earlier Washington houses may have been an even greater incentive.

By early January 1910, Pope had produced a sketch depicting a rather cubic, stone-faced house with lateral projections. This compact mass projected an air of refinement directly related to its antecedent, the Hitt house. As a unit, it was very much in keeping with the sober refinement of the Hitt House, with its tall, narrow proportions and fine details. This design of the central section was followed in subsequent plans, but the landscaping was changed. Pope originally intended to raise the surrounding land to reduce the entrance grade to the house, creating a forecourt defined by dense hedges and enclosed by brick walls and iron fencing. But this scheme made for awkward proportions and was soon altered.

By the end of January, Pope had developed preliminary designs from this sketch, Adamesque in style, featuring a segmental pedimented entrance, Adamesque columns, and garlanded and swagged window cornices. But this design was not to be the final one. In February, the depth of the house was reduced and the wings lengthened, resulting in a much larger house that presented an entirely different image, one whose details were clearly inspired by buildings in Rome.

By June, the general plans for the house were finalized, including a change of exterior materials to brick, and then from dark red brick to the present salmon color. The interior details were a curious composite of Adamesque and modern French motifs. Not surprisingly, this solution was not successful and the interior was redesigned to continue the Roman references of the exterior.

As completed in 1912, the house presents an extremely simple design whose clarity reflects Pope's ability to comprehend the essential nature of a style and then reinterpret it in his own fashion (fig. 3-15). The house was carefully sited on the edge of the hill so that the rear porch and upstairs balconies became intimate extensions of their adjacent spaces with overpowering views of monumental Washington. Its prominence (the ground floor is at least thirty feet above Sixteenth Street) dictated a severe treatment that would project a dignified reserve toward the White House. Pope subordinated the detailing of the house to the geometrically composed, Georgian-inspired mass of the building. In the detailing, however, Pope consulted the sources of Georgian architecture—antique and Renaissance buildings—to re-create the style. The windows were based on Letarouilly's measured drawings of the frieze of the ground-floor court of the Palazzo Farnese. The porte cochère, although original in concept, has a particular Roman feel that is conveyed through the proportions of the columns and the curving entablature (fig. 3-16). The rear porch, commanding a view of Washington, shares the proportions of the colonnade at Peruzzi's Palazzo Massimo alle Colonne in Rome (fig. 3-17).

The interior was designed to meet the entertainment needs of a diplomatic household. The large entrance hall could accommodate huge parties and dictated circulation in a clockwise motion through a series of reception and living rooms that culminated in the dining room. The bold interior detailing again came from various historical sources. The entrance hall's Ionic order was based on that of the Erectheum. The reception and living rooms were strongly Georgian, while the dining room, with its elaborate frieze based on that of the Pantheon, provided a perfect frame for John Singer Sargent's portrait of Mrs. White.

The White house went one step beyond Pope's previous work, in that he managed to dissolve a style into its constituent elements and then re-create it from certain of its original sources. However, Pope's approach to architecture demanded constant attention to form and detail in order to maintain the appropriate balance and prevent them from becoming simply banal. Unfortunately, he could still occasionally produce a dull building, as is well-illustrated in publisher Robert J. Collier Jr.'s house (1911) in Wickatunk, New Jersey, which has been remodeled as a retirement home for nuns (fig 3-18).

In Collier's country house, Pope was faced with the task of providing a building that would simultaneously preserve the intimate feel of a farmhouse and provide adequate space for fifty weekend guests and a great variety of outdoor activities. Pope chose to adapt the basic form of Mount Vernon, and, enlarging on the theme of its porches, used double-height

Fig. 3-16. White house. Entrance facade.

Fig. 3-17. White house. Rear facade.

porticoes to protect slightly recessed ground-level courts, which were considered most practical for the entertainment of hunting parties and riders in general. However, extending Mount Vernon's form to cover a two-hundred-foot-long facade made a pastiche of Pope's choice of models. Due to their relative size, the details and columns failed to hold their own against the immense mass of the building and were overpowered by the expanse of clapboard.

Inherent in this design was the difficult problem of creating a vast yet unostentatious house. Pope's selection of the colonial farmhouse type would seem to have been appropriate, but his specific references to Mount Vernon—most notably the double staircase in the main hall—negate the possibility that the house could appear unpretentious. Pope's arrangement of the rooms, however, was absolutely appropriate, with drawing room and dining room flanking the central stair hall, perfectly placed for entertainment.

1912–19:
AN EXPANDING REPERTOIRE

After the completion of the Henry White house, Pope's domestic commissions increased dramatically. Between 1912 and 1919, with his design of at least thirteen major houses in several different styles, his

reputation as a house designer was solidified. His careful analysis of the principles of a style was not limited to a particular mode. In fact, the choice of style consistently seems to have been a reflection of the client's preference. Thus Pope's houses can be grouped into stylistic types, including the Tudor, Italian Renaissance, colonial revival, and Georgian revival, each one having been subjected to Pope's penetrating stylistic analysis.

In the Levi P. Morton house (1912), on Scott Circle and Massachusetts Avenue in Washington, D.C., Pope transformed an out-of-date residence designed by John Fraser into a thoroughly modern house for the retired diplomat, investment banker, governor of New York, and vice president. Morton, a leading member of Washington society, must have contacted Pope in late 1911 or early 1912. By the end of 1912, Pope had already transformed the house. The brick exterior had been replaced with limestone, and the interior room arrangement was also modified.

While the plan was certainly dictated to some extent by the shape of the original house, the skill of Pope's design lies in his ability to regularize and classicize a building that was originally picturesque in plan and massing. The finished house is based on the forms and decorative elements of Italian palaces of the mid- to late-sixteenth century as well as Parisian *hôtels* of the mid-eighteenth century. However, the

overall scheme is too general to cite specific sources. By judiciously shaving off bow windows and turrets and straightening corners, the massing was made more cubic without any overall loss in space. Despite the apparent irregularities of form, Pope succeeded in developing a floor plan that conformed to his usual formula of a central hall and stairs, with rooms regularly distributed around the periphery. Given the formal austerity of the exterior, the interior was surprisingly decorated in a restrained rococo mode.

At the same time as the Morton house was being remodeled, Pope was designing the Robert S. McCormick house (fig. 3-19), a large dwelling at the other (west) end of Massachusetts Avenue. McCormick was a member of the family that invented the reaper, and had had a successful career as secretary to the American Legation at the Court of St. James, the first American ambassador to Austria-Hungary (1902), and then as ambassador to Russia, in which capacity he was involved in working out a settlement to the Russo-Japanese War (1904–05). In 1905, he was appointed ambassador to France, where he later became an outspoken advocate for a world court system. Recently retired from the diplomatic corps, McCormick may have turned to Pope because of the architect's success with, and recommendations from, his predecessors at the American Embassy in Paris—Henry White and Levi Morton.

The first rendering of McCormick's proposed residence showed a massive Tuscan villa with multiple entrances and a porte cochère with a projecting pavilion facing southeast toward downtown Washington. This projecting pavilion and side entrance were abandoned in the final design in favor of a more cubic scheme whose basic mass was interrupted only by a small garden porch on a minor facade to the south. In style it was based on the Roman palace type of the sixteenth century. The shape of the building subsumed almost all of the decorative elements within its mass, with the exception of the porch. The Tuscan-columned entrance is based on that of the Peruzzi's Palazzo Massimo, while the medallions and cartouches in the window spandrels and the belt course decoration appear to be derived from the Palazzo Farnese (now the French Embassy in Rome)—a fitting source for the home of a former ambassador to France. The result is a stolid and distant image of reserved elegance that still dominates its portion of Massachusetts Avenue. In the interior, on the ground floor, a semicircular staircase (fig. 3-20) with a rococo balustrade leads up from a large entrance hall decorated with Corinthian pilasters based on early Florentine Renaissance examples and uncharacteristically deep plaster reliefs whose style is almost rococo. The first floor comprised a series of eclectic exercises in the Tudor style (pantry), the Georgian and French

Fig. 3-19. Robert S. McCormick house, Washington, D.C., 1912. (Now the Brazilian ambassador's residence.)

Fig. 3-20

Fig. 3-20.
McCormick house.
Main staircase.

Fig. 3-21.
McCormick house.
Large drawing room.

Fig. 3-22.
McCormick house.
Salon.

Fig. 3-21

Fig. 3-22

Fig. 3-23

Fig. 3-24

rococo styles (small drawing room), the rococo (large drawing room, fig. 3-21), and again the Georgian (dining room, fig. 3-22), creating an opulent yet confused effect in sharp contrast to the austerity of the exterior.

The Tudor

While Pope had briefly experimented with the Norman variant of northern Renaissance styles, the next commission that demanded a northern Renaissance style was a Park Avenue town house (begun 1910) in New York for the literary and theatrical couple Reginald and Anna De Koven, who engaged Pope to design a residence in the Tudor-Jacobean manner. The result was a house whose exterior was tightly composed and whose detailing was of an even, consonant tone. Bricks were laid in Flemish bond, with headers creating a diaper pattern. For all its style, the house—essentially a London townhouse with applied oriels—has a very cold appearance. The plan was very similar to that of the Hitt house, except that the second floor was composed of two large rooms to accommodate the De Kovens' Sunday musicales. The interior decoration was one of Pope's most derivative. Ceiling and wainscotting were directly quoted from the palace of Bromley-by-Bow (1606). The staircase was a reconstruction of that at Knole House (1605) in Kent, while the plaster ceiling in the great hall of the second floor was borrowed from a seventeenth-century inn in Banbury. The paneling of the reception room was taken from a house in Utrecht, while a screen in the great hall was taken from a seventeenth-century Swiss convent. As Pope's first major design in this style, the house shows promise, but the interior was clearly among Pope's most inconsistent.

The Stuart Duncan House in Newport, known as Bonniecrest (1912–14; converted to condominiums, grounds covered with buildings) expands Pope's repertoire of country house styles to the Tudor, a style that he would later use for his own house in Newport.

Stuart Duncan was a midwestern banker and manufacturer who, although he may have expressed a preference for the Tudor style, probably left the choice of specific historic paradigm—the Warwickshire manor of Compton Wynyates (1520)—to Pope. While the design of the house appears to owe much to Compton, relatively little was directly derived from the manor; rather, Pope's Duncan estate is a carefully-controlled synthesis of American picturesque design principles found in the shingle style, and academically correct decorative elements borrowed from Compton. The resultant image is one of controlled elegance that mediates between the Olmsted-designed greensward of the inland and the rocky shore of Brenton Cove (fig. 3-23).

Fig. 3-25

*Fig. 3-23.
Bonniecrest (Stuart Duncan house), Newport, Rhode Island, 1912–14.*

*Fig. 3-24.
Bonniecrest.
Entrance facade.*

*Fig. 3-25.
Bonniecrest. Detail of entryway showing brick diaper work.*

Abandoning the traditional Tudor courtyard plan as inappropriate to a site with magnificent vistas and breezes, Pope instead chose a linear dogleg plan organized around a two-hundred-foot-long gallery that links all of the public rooms. On the exterior, the only overt borrowing from Compton Wynyates was its famous entrance (fig. 3-24), a two-story buttressed pavilion enframing a pointed Tudor entryway completed with crenellation and brick diaper work (fig. 3-25). On the interior (fig. 3-26), however, Pope's motifs were based on those of Compton Wynyates among various other sources. The door and paneling of the dining room were modeled on the screen in the Great Hall of Compton; the library mantelpiece was taken from a fifteenth-century house; a Tudor-style screen between the gallery and dining room was created by master blacksmith Samuel Yellin; and all of the plasterwork and paneling was based on other Tudor sources. To complete this romantic image, the furnishings were designed in an appropriately sympathetic style, and included imported antiques and reproductions of objects in the Victoria and Albert Museum. To give the house an illusion and patina of age, every effort was made to distress the materials. Exterior stonework was sandblasted and beaten with chains. The copper gutters and leaders were specially treated to simulate weathering and oxidation, and interior woodwork was bathed with solvents and purposely marred. The slate roof was given the look of age through the use of slate split from the outside surfaces of the bed, which is usually of extremely uneven color, thickness, and texture. Only by using this whole array of effects had Pope avoided the jarring sense of newness found in so many Tudor revival houses.

From a modernist point of view, what made this house successful was that Pope had once again mastered the shapes and textures of a particular style. He employed deceptive measures to create a building that appears to have evolved organically over time, but was in fact intentionally composed all at once using discrete, archaeologically correct stylistic elements that were combined to produce a synthetic impression of picturesque elegance.

Pope also demonstrated his facility with this style in the country house for Virginia Graham Fair Vanderbilt (1911) in Old Westbury, New York (fig. 3-27). When the Vanderbilts became estranged in 1911, Pope was hired to design a new country house for "Bertie." Reflecting her Francophile tastes, he obligingly produced a clinically academic Norman half-timber dwelling on a somewhat regularized dogleg plan. In a predictably Beaux-Arts-inspired manner, the picturesque elements were placed into a regular rhythm, in which they appeared at calculated intervals. The dogleg plan provides a picturesque framework on which to hang all of the components of the style.

Fig. 3-26.
Bonniecrest.
Living room.

Fig. 3-27

Fig. 3-27. Virginia
Graham Fair
Vanderbilt house,
Old Westbury,
New York, 1911.

Fig. 3-28. Kamp Kill
Kare (renovation
for Francis Patrick
Garvan), near
Raquette Lake,
New York, 1915–17.

Fig. 3-29. Kamp Kill
Kare. Main house.

Fig. 3-28

Fig. 3-29

The Adirondack Camp

Although Pope continued to design Tudor-style houses until 1920, he was also involved with a particularly American house type during this period: the Adirondack camp. In 1914, New York attorney and silver and furniture collector Francis Patrick Garvan purchased Kamp Kill Kare, located near Raquette Lake, New York. Originally built in the early 1880s, the complex burned down in 1915, and Garvan, who previously had used Pope for the renovation of the kitchen in his Long Island home, hired him to rebuild it.

Pope's particular contribution was the imposition of order on the picturesque form of the Adirondack camp. A large tower announces the entrance through the service yard (fig. 3-28). From there, the road leads down toward the water and the long main house (fig. 3-29), whose dogleg plan is familiar from Pope's earlier designs. With this plan controlling the overall form of the building, picturesque elements appear at carefully planned and rhythmic intervals. The composition terminates in a large boathouse, whose decoration marked the final instance of a series of porches and gables. The great surprise of the panorama of the camp is the chapel (fig. 3-30). Originally conceived as a massive, low-towered structure in the vein of a rural medieval country parish church connected to the mass of the main building, it was pared down to become a simpler Romanesque-inspired element.

The interiors of Garvan's Kill Kare evoked fantastic visions of cavernous monumental halls enlivened and made more mystifying by complex trusses, elaborate stone fireplaces, and rustic furniture (fig. 3-31). Much of this atmosphere, however, was the result of the translation of Pope's sketches into wood by local craftsmen, who possessed a less disciplined approach to the decoration of the interior than Pope had planned in the original drawings. Still, Kamp Kill Kare gives us a first glimpse of Pope's interpretation of a genuinely American style.

The Adamesque

The Myers, Frick, Burden, and Mills houses, all completed by 1915, were further demonstrations of Pope's reductionist restatements of the Adamesque style and its American interpretations. Pope and his contemporaries seem to have attached nationalistic associations to this style. Pope himself clearly associated it with colonial architecture of the South. This sentiment may have been reinforced by the fact that the style was first prominent in America just after the Revolution, and was possibly seen by Pope as the country's first domestic architecture in the classical idiom. Whatever his inspiration, he produced four compelling examples in the Adamesque mode.

Fig. 3-30

Fig. 3-31

Fig. 3-30. *Kamp Kill Kare. Sketch of chapel.*

Fig. 3-31. *Kamp Kill Kare. Sketch of interior.*

Fig. 3-35

Fig. 3-36

continued some of the trends he initiated in the Myers house, but relied more on British precedent, or rather omitted the allusion to American architecture.

Dominating the main entrance to the suburban development, the building occupies a central position toward the rear of the property while a brick wall surrounds the site. To accentuate the primacy of the building, the southern garden facade curves outward (fig. 3-35), echoing the shape of the site. To maintain privacy, Pope placed the building perpendicular to the entrance drive, thereby creating a private forecourt framed on the northern side by a decorated garage wall. The north or entrance facade (figs. 3-36, 3-38, 3-39) presents surprising variety in volume. A recessed entrance echoes the bowed south facade, and its giant order again speaks of a dual heritage, American and British.

In plan, the house was typical of most of Pope's works. Its disposition of rooms (fig. 3-37) was a simple cruciform with a large entry hall (fig. 3-40) surrounded by smaller rooms. The upper floors were planned as simple double loaded corridors flanked by bedrooms and private sitting rooms.

Although the interior decoration of the house was described as Greek revival by contemporaries, the scheme for the entryway actually appears to have been based on Adam's proposal for Luton Hoo (1768–75) in Bedfordshire. The library (fig. 3-41) may have been derived from Bowood in Wiltshire, built in various stages from the 1760s to 1834, with Henry Holland, Robert Adam, and Charles Barry as architects. The mantels in each of the rooms were taken from the Fricks' former house in Baltimore, but were well integrated into the decorative scheme. In the overall unity of the design, created by the proportion and mass of the building, Pope had arrived at a general formula for this style, which could be altered slightly to create seemingly novel permutations based on a repertory of preexisting forms.

Although the line and mass of the Arthur Scott Burden (later Mrs. Guy Fairfax Cary) house (1915, destroyed) in Jericho, Long Island, differs greatly from that of the Frick and Myers houses, it shares with them certain details in ornament—most notably the pilaster order and cornice topped by a parapet. This provides a well-proportioned foil to the oversized, floor-to-ceiling windows of both stories, which were necessary to capture sufficient northern light to illuminate an interior hall painted in shades of gray and slate in the manner of an Adamesque town house. The open-bed, pedimented front doorway with blind fanlight provides a strong decorative element at the apparent center of the composition, while an extensive garden, hidden by low walls and a loggia, lent visual balance to the rear of the house (fig. 3-42).

The interior layout followed Pope's customary scheme of an entry hall mediating between the cool

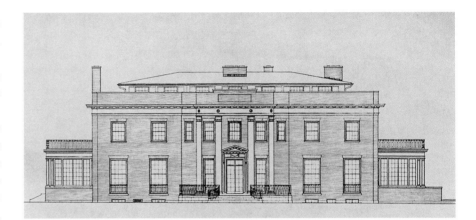

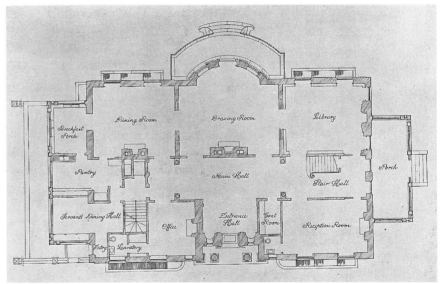

Fig. 3-37

Fig. 3-35. Charlcote (James Swan Frick house), Baltimore, Maryland, 1914. Garden facade.

Fig. 3-36. Charlcote. Entrance facade.

Fig. 3-37. Charlcote. Elevation and plan.

Fig. 3-38. Charlcote.
Detail of entrance
facade.

Fig. 3-39. Charlcote.
Detail of column
capital.

Fig. 3-40. Charlcote.
Entry hall.

Fig. 3-41. Charlcote.
Library.

Fig. 3-42

northern entrance and the more warmly decorated living spaces. However, the elliptical staircase and stairway hall thrusting dramatically into the simple rectangular space, along with the curving entablature enliven his rather sedate entry hall without disrupting its symmetry and proportion. The living spaces, painted in shades of olive green and yellow, were restrained, with Adamesque pilasters and simply paneled walls to set off the period furniture (figs. 3-43, 3-44).

The distinguishing features of the Burden house are its size and adaptation to the landscape: well-removed from the rest of the world on its seventy suburban acres, the house achieved the impression of privacy coupled with a sense of age implied by the slightly rambling servants' quarters. This small feature moved critic Augusta Owen Patterson to write that the house was "as near to being an old English manor house as almost anything in this country." Her praise for Pope and his work was lavish, and she termed the Burden house as "nearly perfect for purposes which the modern American country house is planned to serve as anything can be" (*American Homes of Today*, 87, 1924). In her eyes, Pope could hardly do better, and he himself may have been of the same opinion, for he would soon abandon the style.

The Ogden Mills house (1915) in Woodbury, Long Island, was Pope's final country house design in the Adamesque mode. Built for a secretary of the United States Treasury, this residence of imperial dignity was neither extravagant nor ostentatious in its detail or material, but achieved a surprising monumentality through massing and decoration (figs. 3-45, 3-46).

Here again, Pope chose to spread the plan over a low plateau and to provide views in all directions. He selected an H-plan, which ensured that the house would be flooded with light and would not appear rambling and ill-organized. He also used a massing parti similar to that of the Charles Gould house for this project, resulting in a two-story central block flanked by one-story wings.

To hold its own in relation to the volume of the house, the decorative scheme, consisting of the Adamesque order drawn from the portico facade at Bowood, was given depth, and appears as an attached order. The decorative scheme is further augmented by niches with Adamesque urns, plaques, and blind arches with swagging. Even in conjunction with the order, these barely soften the stark walls of this composition, although the severe image is eased by large open loggias on the south side. It is no surprise to find that the building was soon heavily covered with ivy as a means of mitigating the severity of Pope's composition.

The plan is remarkably similar to that of the Arthur Scott Burden house, and, to some extent, the Henry White house as well. An entrance hall and

Fig. 3-43

Fig. 3-44

Fig. 3-42. *Arthur Scott Burden house, Jericho, New York, 1915. Rear facade.*

Figs. 3-43, 3-44. *Burden house. Interior views.*

adjoining stairway hall with elliptical staircase mediate between the exterior and the public rooms, once again arranged on a U-plan. Guest rooms form the western wing of the entrance court, while the service area completes the front court and functions as a screen for the separate service yard. This solution also provided for a service core near the dining area. The upper floor was planned in a straightforward manner. Unfortunately, photographs of the interiors were never published, preventing a fuller assessment of the house.

It was the overwhelming sense of massiveness that created the lasting impression of the Mills house. In combination with the severe refinement of detail that makes this work successful, the emphasis on mass, proportion, and understated detail provided Pope's client with a stolid, conservative architectural vocabulary.

That Pope soon abandoned the Adamesque style would seem to indicate he had taken it as far as he could: the ten-year exercise in refinement had finally reached its limit; no further variants could be conceived. Had Pope created something particularly American? The English journal *Architectural Review* thought so, and published his four Adamesque houses as excellent examples of American domestic architecture. Although the French government awarded Pope the Legion of Honor for the design of the Arthur Scott Burden house, at this point he would seek another, more robust style to meet his clients' needs—the early Georgian.

The Georgian

The Georgian style appealed to Pope's clients through its association with eighteenth-century English gentry, the house being connected with the grand manner of life in this milieu. The appeal to Pope would have been that the essential components of the style were codified, yet it allowed a certain freedom of composition, since his creative strength lay in manipulating styles that permitted reduction into essential components and then reinvention. Furthermore, the American variants of the Georgian style were thought to be the first truly original American architecture. Whatever the motivation, Pope would continue to work primarily within this tradition into the early 1930s.

The William F. Hencken house, known as Merleigh Farm (1917), in Greenwich, Connecticut, was one of Pope's first full-fledged essays in the Georgian style. It was a rather free translation of the English country house of the mid- to late eighteenth century. The hilly topography of the site dictated that the house turn its back on the approach road, so that the garden facade became the most prominent, and consequently, the most imposing main facade. Its outline was emphasized with a simple cornice atop

a slightly projecting central pavilion. This exterior relied on second quality bricks, laid in Flemish bond with dark headers to provide a broad color treatment to the virtually unadorned wall. Quoining, a stringcourse, and a mouse-tooth cornice provide only the slightest relief from the extreme simplicity of the mass. This deliberate emphasis on simplicity in turn highlighted the simple stone entrance, accentuating the bold force of the Tuscan order and the pulvinated frieze.

The plan, based on the Georgian central hall format, was organized along Pope's standard lines. The interior was as restrained as the exterior, and all decorative elements were extremely simple expressions of the Georgian. The most dramatic element was a swagged frieze in the central hall, the rest of the rooms being decorated with very plain cornices.

As he did so successfully with the Adam style, Pope synthesized English Georgian into something utterly distinct from its antecedents. In the blunt and basic austerity of this example one can understand Pope's intention with his subsequent interpretations of the Georgian: to use it as a simple and more direct expression of the conservative and relatively informal lives of his country house clients.

Two houses begun as early as 1917 further elucidate this aspect of Pope's work. One, the J. Randolph Robinson house in Westbury, New York, is clearly American in origin; the other, the Andrew Varick Stout house in Red Bank, New Jersey, is inspired exclusively by English precedents.

In the Robinson house, Pope further experimented with the Mount Vernon model. The entrance facade, with a great portico and recessed wings, presents a more successful and liberal adaptation of the paradigm than his earlier attempts. The garden facade was freely composed, with a pair of projecting bays flanking a central Palladian window. The interior organization departs from Pope's typical compact plan. The stairway hall copies one half of the double stair at Mount Vernon, and is overwhelmed by adjoining rooms, creating an excessively tight entry. Given the unsuccessful floor plan, it is no surprise that Pope, probably finding Mount Vernon too restrictive as a model, abandoned the form and looked to more articulated models of the American colonial house whose proportions would still be pleasing on a large scale.

The house for Andrew Varick Stout was much more successful. The exterior (fig. 3-47), based on a rural house on Downing Street in Farnham, Surrey, which Pope would have seen on one of his many visits to England, maintains its sturdy proportions even when dramatically increased in size to meet the needs of modern country life. The deep parapet with recessed spandrels provides an adequate visual support for the elaborate cornices at the main and garden entrances. These doorways and their cornices offer

Figs. 3-47–3-49.
Andrew Varick Stout
house, Red Bank,
New Jersey, 1917.

a robust contrast to the planar emphasis of the house, while the depth of carving acts as a foil to the solidity of the structure, as does the arched, covered porch.

The plan follows Pope's usual pattern with a large entry hall mediating between the major spaces. The decoration, executed in a delicate late-Georgian manner, acts as a foil to the robust exterior. This house follows in the tradition of Pope's Adamesque brick houses but is sturdier and bolder.

In the Thomas Frothingham house (1919–21, later owned by the Sloan family and now the United States Golf Association museum), in Far Hills, New Jersey, Pope's Georgian experiments took a decidedly chauvinistic turn. Basing the design on the Maryland five-part plan houses such as Whitehall, Mount Airy, or Sabine Hall, Pope merely enlarged the scale and adapted the formula slightly to comply with Frothingham's needs. The main body of the house (figs. 3-50, 3-51) follows Pope's standard formula, but the ground floor of the western dependency was designed as a separate living room. This separation of entertainment spaces seems ill-considered, but may have been conceived to take advantage of the fact that the land slopes off to the west, providing distant vistas of adjacent farmland. With the exception of the familiar curving stair (fig. 3-52), the Frothingham house interiors were relatively sparse. The library contained the obligatory paneling taken from an eighteenth-century English house, while the dining room was decorated

Fig. 3-50. Thomas Frothingham house, Far Hills, New Jersey, 1919–21.

Fig. 3-51. Frothingham house. Detail of entrance portico.

Fig. 3-52

86   RESIDENTIAL ARCHITECTURE

Fig. 3-53

Fig. 3-52.
Frothingham house.
Main staircase.

Fig. 3-53.
Frothingham house.
Detail of chimney-
breast in dining
room.

with a fretwork frieze and prominent Georgian chimney-breast (fig. 3-53).

The most important aspect of this house was Pope's decision to abandon English prototypes and adapt an American house type. In an elaborate discussion of the project for the magazine *Country Life* (October 1920), he set out his principles for planning outbuildings, demonstrating his understanding of the workings of country house life and the place of servants in this social hierarchy. Accordingly, stables, cow barns, and garages were composed into a series of open courtyards, which were surrounded by an orchard and well removed from the main house. In a rare statement, Pope justified the use of these forms, finding great appeal in the particularly American qualities of the form:

> One is struck most of all, in studying the plans of this house and estate, with the successful embodiment in it of the old simple American traditions of building. No attempt has been made to create one of those familiar show places which, by the perfection of their cleverly antiqued half-timbering and Tudor chimneys, compete for admiration with the exotic magnificence of the French chateau next door. It is, rather, the healthy symbol of American race consciousness and pride in the achievements of our own people, intensified since the Great War, which has brought with it the realization that the mode of building that took form in this country contemporaneously with our own development into a separate people, is the most nearly perfect expression that has been devised of the traits of character and mode of life that we like to call American.

In Pope's disciplined use of historical precedent and his virtual reconstruction of styles from first principles, he develops a particularly American classicism. Starting from an urge to create something specifically appropriate to the United States, he drew upon the accepted canons and icons of architecture, creating a style appropriate to American tastes, which at the time valorized refined, severe understatement.

French Revivals

Pope was also willing to design in such revival and other eclectic styles, and created dignified houses based on a variety of sources including chateaux of the sixteenth through eighteenth centuries. While in

Fig. 3-54

Fig. 3-55

general, after about 1910, such houses were not popular with most country house clients, certain aspects of French architecture of the eighteenth century still interested some of Pope's urban clientele.

The house for the widow of Pittsburgh iron baron William B. Leeds and her husband, Prince Christopher of Greece (1915), on Fifth Avenue between Ninety-sixth and Ninety-seventh streets in New York, was probably Pope's first effort in this French style (fig. 3-54). He devised a scheme whereby the house turned its back on Fifth Avenue, with the entrance porte cochère being reached by a narrow driveway between two buildings. This massing owes much to Pope's own designs for the James Swan Frick house, but it also recalls the Château de Champs and Château d'Agnes, small early eighteenth-century houses near Paris, as well as Blondel's project for a country house in his *De la distribution des maisons de plaisance* (1738). It also seems a tamer version of Horace Trumbauer's Elms of fifteen years earlier in Newport.

In the plan (fig. 3-55), Pope further asserted his formula. Using Blondel's project and Château de Champs as his guide, he gave the most important rooms views of the gardens and Fifth Avenue, and placed a vertical service core in one corner near the dining room, so that service could be performed with a minimum of contact with the owners or their guests. Pope seemed to take great pride in the project, for he exhibited the drawings three years later at the Annual Exhibition of the Architectural League.

Nevertheless, his excursions into French eighteenth-century styles were infrequent. One of the few was his final involvement on Washington's Meridian Hill, which marked the completion of building on the knoll adjoining the Henry White house. Irwin Boyle Laughlin, diplomat, member of a Pittsburgh steel family, and friend of Henry White, purchased the land in 1912. But it was not until his first retirement from the diplomatic corps in 1919 that he approached Pope to design a house for him. Being a noted Francophile and avid collector of eighteenth-century French furniture and paintings, it is no surprise that Laughlin wanted his house designed in a French style. Pope obligingly developed his own interpretation of a French chateau which was clearly informed by such eighteenth-century country and city residences in and around Paris as La Chesnaie, Champs, Maisons, and the Hôtel de Bouillon (now the École des Beaux-Arts).

By August 1920, the plans for the Laughlin house were finalized, and construction was completed in 1922. The facade (fig. 3-56), a vision of staid formality, sets the stage for an imposing interior. Just as he had done in the White house, Pope achieved a particular synthesis of a style, this time evoking an external vision that matched the current definition of the Louis XVI style. The solemn mass of the house is broken only by the symmetrical projecting

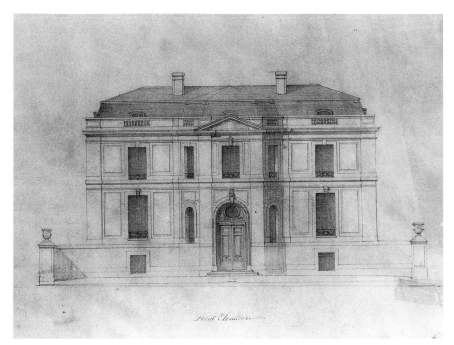

Fig. 3-56

volumes that provide access and egress. The rhythm of the fenestration, interrupted on the interior due to the necessity of hanging extremely large works of art on the walls, is maintained on the exterior by blind windows.

The grand entrance provided a transitional space between the reserved exterior and the more opulent interior. In a manner similar to that of Blondel, of Champs, and of Pope's own project for Prince Christopher, this main floor is organized around a single central gallery whose elaborate interior decoration sets the tone for the rest of the house. The simply decorated, intimate library needed the least direct light and thus was located on the northeast corner; the gracious drawing room was situated on the southeast; the solarium, whose airy vision draws the visitor well into the foyer, was placed at the center; and the dining room was located on southwest to draw the low golden light of evening and to serve as a setting for a large tapestry.

Views from the Laughlin house and garden were carefully dictated by Pope's placement of fountains and sculptural elements, which ensured that one focused first on nearby elements and then out to the skyline of Washington. In his approach to landscape design, Pope considered spaces adjacent to the house as intimate outdoor extensions of it (fig. 3-57), while the distant landscape was treated as a series of vistas serving as focal points from which one viewed the house, and to which one's eye drifted from inside the house, resulting in a very carefully controlled series of partial views of the house.

Pope's use of the French style was met with great approval, and thus it is especially curious that, having designed what was considered to be a modern paradigm in the Laughlin house, he rarely attempted or was asked to attempt another house in this style.

Fig. 3-54. Proposal for house of Prince Christopher of Greece (unbuilt), New York, 1915.

Fig. 3-55. Proposal for house of Prince Christopher of Greece (unbuilt). Plan.

Fig. 3-56. Irwin Boyle Laughlin house, Washington, D.C., 1919–22. Elevation.

Fig. 3-57

Fig. 3-58

1920–25: GEORGIAN ASCENDANT

The period 1912 to 1919 saw a dramatic increase in Pope's residential work, and likewise was distinguished by a level of quality that remained very high. By 1920, *Country Life* magazine had recognized him as one of the best country house architects in America. His work in the early 1920s seems to have changed focus only slightly, and essentially followed national trends, which saw fewer and smaller country estates being undertaken and the same range of styles being selected, if perhaps with a slight shift in favor of American variants of Georgian styles.

Although Pope rarely designed houses outside his established architectural vocabulary, the Joseph Knapp house, known as Tenacre (c. 1920–22), in Southampton, New York, is an example of a successful departure (fig. 3-58). The interior planning represents a scaled-down version of Pope's customary parti, but the exterior returns to the shingle style of his mentor McKim. The scale of the house and its location among the dunes of Long Island may have suggested an informal treatment. A romantically sloping gable and a flowing plastic membrane of shingles are held in compositional check by the symmetry of the massing and the compact organization of the plan.

For most of his other minor commissions, Pope returned to American variants of the Georgian style. However, in each case he adapted it to fit the local vernacular. Two examples of this are the J. H. Carstairs house (c. 1924) in Ardmore, Pennsylvania, and the John F. Wilkins house (1923–24, extant

remains incorporated into a cemetery) in Rockville, Maryland, in which Pope used the stone vernacular of the Pennsylvania Georgian-style farmhouse in combination with a variant on the Maryland five-part plans as his point of departure.

Accordingly, the Carstairs house, composed of rough dressed, whitewashed stone, was Georgian in massing with minimal detail. The exterior expressed overt references to the Georgian, including a modillioned eave and Chippendale muntins in the dormers. The interior treatment, where modillioned cornices and segmental pedimented overdoors were used, was more overtly derived from the mid-eighteenth century, occasioning an unsettling contrast between the severe exterior and rich interior.

The Wilkins house is a variation on Pope's Frothingham/Sloan house. It is unassuming, but the entryway, adorned with a carefully finished segmental-arched pediment, stands in excessive contrast to the rough dressed ashlar masonry of the building. A Palladian window at the rear and the porch trellises can be faulted for the same reason. The house followed Pope's by now formulaic country house plan, and was decorated in an understated Georgian manner.

Between 1920 and 1930, Pope's most ambitious residential project, the Marshall Field II estate, known as Caumsett, was conceived, designed, and built on Lloyd Neck in Huntington on Long Island's North Shore. Although not innovative, Caumsett is extremely important because it represents the culmination of all the design techniques Pope had developed over the previous twenty-five years.

The commission was awarded soon after Field, the midwestern publisher and notorious Anglophile, purchased 1,750 acres on Lloyd Neck with the idea of creating a self-sufficient rural estate in the British

Fig. 3-57. *Laughlin house. Garden facade.*

Fig. 3-58. *Tenacre (Joseph Knapp house), Southampton, New York, c. 1920–22.*

Fig. 3-63. Caumsett.
Barn.

Fig. 3-64. Caumsett.
Plan of main house.

Figs. 3-65, 3-66.
Caumsett. Main house.

Fig. 3-63

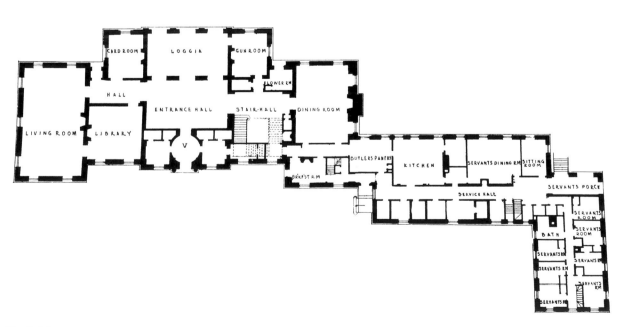

Fig. 3-64

Fig. 3-65

Fig. 3-66

Surrey (1760–76). The main house was organized according to the typical Pope formula, with a centrally placed great hall and adjoining stairway hall. A vast L-shaped service wing (now destroyed) trailed off to the east of the main building.

The interiors perpetrated the image of a late-seventeenth-century English house. Rooms were designed around paneling that Mrs. Field had purchased from various American and English houses, which necessitated in one case altering the room heights of an entire floor.

The architectural press devoted much space but little critical comment to the project. The vastness of the undertaking seemed to overshadow its architectural import, and the critics were more interested in the marshalling of talent and resources required for such a large project than in the actual design of the buildings. When evaluated in relation to Pope's other projects, the commission is merely a massive application of the same design and planning principles used in all of his country houses.

While Pope was finalizing the design of Caumsett, he began the design of the Moses Taylor house (1922–27) near Newport. The idea for the style of this house, also known as Glen Farm, came from Mrs. Taylor, who had spent much time in France and had a penchant for the chateau type. The low-lying site on a strip of land along the Sakonnet River led Pope to choose a Loire valley prototype. But since the approach to the property was from higher ground, and the first views of the house would be from above, Pope settled on the much desired peaked-roof French manor house type (figs. 3-69–3-71). The result was a greatly enlarged version of Les Grotteaux.

In his usual manner, Pope distilled from this elaborate stucco- and sandstone-faced mass a grouping of simplified volumes (figs. 3-72, 3-73). Again, he applied hierarchic planning principles to create an ordered image for a type of house that was traditionally loosely planned and appropriately picturesque. Each of the three groupings of hipped roofs cover separate sections of the house: the service rooms, the central reception rooms (fig. 3-74), and the large living room and porch.

In plan, the house follows Pope's canonical formula, with a large hall separating the principal public spaces. The interior finishes are aggressive borrowings from eighteenth-century French examples in the style of Louis XV. In formal composition and feeling, this house is an expanded and more fully conceived version of the Charles Gould house, Chateauiver. Although Glen Farm lacks the severity of Chateauiver, it demonstrates again a distillation of a style into its essential elements, whose picturesque nature is carefully controlled and expressed in a measured manner. In comparison to the similarly styled Otto Kahn estate in Huntington, Long Island

Figs. 3-67, 3-68. Caumsett. Renderings of main house.

Fig. 3-69

Fig. 3-70

Fig. 3-71

(Delano & Aldrich, 1917–1930s), Pope's design is more carefully composed. The horizontal emphasis of the massing is perfect for its low site along the river, while the vertical emphasis of the Delano & Aldrich scheme is out of keeping with the flat terrain of Long Island.

1925–37: THE CASTLE OF INDOLENCE

With the first commissions of the years 1925 to 1930, Pope appears to have been working to create something new with an American-based vocabulary of form and materials. By the second half of the 1920s, the appeal of the colonial had reached an almost patriotic fervor. And although Pope's interest in American forms followed the national trend, there also seems to have been a more personal aspect to his interest in colonial forms. He demonstrated an intimate knowledge of the style, on which he imposed his own design criteria, creating a distillation of the lessons of the past which was instilled with reserved emotion.

Between 1925 and 1930, most of the firm's domestic work was for country dwellings. The Southampton hunting box (fig. 3-75) for Standard Oil heir Colonel H. H. Rogers (1926), known as the

Port of the Missing Men, represents one avenue of Pope's experimentation with American colonial vernacular forms. In this case, Pope and his client chose to begin with a preexisting seventeenth-century saltbox, which was expanded into a large structure whose central spine, in conjunction with a series of gabled pavilions, forms a skewed H-plan, facing a pond. The house was intended as a setting for the client's extensive collection of ship models and American nautical artifacts, and followed a predictable formula in staggering the arrangement of wings along this grand spine to give the impression of a series of structures built over time. In the Port of the Missing Men, Pope was, in a sense, remaking American architecture by creating a grandiose, classicized order from relatively simple, indigenous forms employed in unexpected ways. The interiors reflected a similar affinity for the Early American vernacular forms.

Pope continued this exploration of Early American styles in his design for Brookwood (c. 1927), in Far Hills, New Jersey, for the Frelinghuysen family. In this case, he created a large federal revival house as a setting for the reuse of older architectural elements and individual pieces of family furniture that had been passed down through the family.

The H. W. Lowe House, known as Mariemont (1927), in Wheatley Hills, Long Island, represents a composite of New England and mid-Atlantic federal

Figs. 3-69, 3-70. Glen Farm (Moses Taylor house), near Newport, Rhode Island, 1922–27.

Fig. 3-71. Glen Farm. Rendering.

Figs. 3-72, 3-73.
Glen Farm. Views
of portico.

Fig. 3-74

forms. The ground plan is a variant on the Maryland five-part plan, while the interior articulation of rooms, including the semicircular thrust of the main staircase, follows Pope's typical pattern. The interior decoration, with its chaste Adamesque detailing, maintains a tone consonant with the sparse exterior.

Most of Pope's commissions over the next years required the use of more imposing modes, beginning with the Grosse Pointe, Michigan, home of Roy D. Chapin (1927), president of the Hudson Motor Car Company. Using a slight variation on the massing of the Henry White house, Pope concocted a composite of late Georgian and federal forms. With its Georgian doorway and pilastered Ionic order, the exterior owed much to such late-eighteenth-century tidewater plantations as Nanzatico in King George County, Virginia. Prior to its 1956 remodeling by Anne Ford, only one interior view of the house was published. The decorative scheme was bold and Georgian in detail, but little is known of the plan.

Woodend (1927, now a nature center operated by the Audubon Society), built in Chevy Chase, Maryland, for Captain Chester Wells and his wife, Marion, is a more formal variation on the H-plan. Descended from the design for the Marshall Field house, Woodend is based on a simple and fairly successful scheme in which the massing and exterior decoration complement one another (fig. 3-76). The quoining, balustrade, stone parapet, strong door pediments, and stringcourse enliven the blocky brick exterior. The interior, however, is an unfortunate exercise in disjointed planning of a kind rarely found in Pope's work. But despite these planning defects, the Georgian mouldings and other decorative details of the interior (fig. 3-77) are deftly reproduced.

In the late 1920s, Pope completed a few more Tudor-style houses. The most ambitious of these was Skylands Farm (1924–28, extant) in the Ramapo Mountains along the New York–New Jersey border near Sterlington, New York, and Ringwood, New Jersey (fig. 3-78). Uncharacteristically, Pope relinquished most of the control over this twelve-hundred-acre estate and farm to others: the landscape to the firm of Vitale and Geifert and the interiors to White Allom & Co. The success of the convoluted plan is questionable. The entry and stairway hall seem niggling in comparison to the size of the coat rooms, while the great hall and stairway hall provide the visitor with the only direct access to the dining room. The other major spaces were set off from one another by a series of seemingly unnecessary halls and small hexagonal rooms. The upper two floors with their ten bedrooms are rather unremarkable in plan, consisting of double-loaded corridors. The interiors, a rich, eclectic, and opulent composite of Georgian and Tudor elements, may reflect the efforts of White Allom, but in any case, the Georgian style was carefully allotted to the north wing where the living room and office were located. The separation of these rooms from the others allowed for the transition to another style, and imputed the effect of age to the whole design, in that the shift in style implied a passage of time between the construction of the body of the house and the north wing. With the completion of Skylands, Pope's firm began to quote its own work aggressively, a dangerous trend that often leads to stagnation of design.

The George Sicard house (1927) in Larchmont, New York, was a picturesque fabrication that borrowed from a variety of English Tudor vernacular sources. The main facade was controlled and balanced by two pavilions, one advancing and one receding, which framed the central entrance. In creating the lush exterior fabric, Pope relied on a

Fig. 3-74. Glen Farm. Reception room.

Fig. 3-75. Port of the Missing Men (Col. H. H. Rogers house), Southampton, New York, 1926.

Fig. 3-75

103

Fig. 3-76

Fig. 3-76. Woodend
(Captain Chester
Wells house), Chevy
Chase, Maryland,
1927.

Fig. 3-77. Woodend.
Entrance hall.

Fig. 3-78. Skylands
Farm (Clarence
Lewis house), near
Sterlington, New
York, and Ringwood,
New Jersey, 1924–28.

Fig. 3-77

combination of rough ashlar limestone and culled clinker bricks to bring a coloristic depth to the wall. In plan, Pope varied his typical formula slightly to ensure that all of the public spaces faced Long Island Sound. Consequently, these rooms are arranged in a stepped diagonal fashion along the southern shore. The interiors were consistently early English Renaissance in style, with simply paneled rooms, lead casement windows, and heavy timber ceilings. It is apparent here that there has been little advancement over earlier houses of the same type, the type having by now become a formula for Pope.

In Pope's own country house, known as The Waves (1928, exterior extant), in Newport, Rhode Island, one again sees a reversion to one of his previously used styles. With an exterior designed in the Tudor style (figs. 3-79, 3-80), the house was laid out in a dogleg U-plan that intentionally conformed to the foundations of the previous house on the site, Lipperts Castle. As with Pope's other Tudor designs, there is a predictable order and rhythm in the arrangement of the decorative elements, such as half-timbering, dormers, and chimney pots. The interiors, however, are entirely Georgian in detail and scale (figs. 3-81–3-83). In a situation where Tudor was the only style that would

match the rambling foundations, Georgian interiors and furnishings were used in this unabashedly eclectic program.

While the major focus of Pope's work remained suburban and country houses, the residences he designed in New York included a very large apartment for Harold C. Richard (c. 1930). Its living and dining rooms were Georgian, the library was Jacobean, faced with Old English wood paneling, and the remaining rooms included a Louis XV master bedroom and boudoir, a bathroom designed in the Directoire style, with playrooms and other bedrooms based on colonial sources. When exhibited at the Architectural League Annual Exhibition, the apartment was described by George S. Chappell in *The Architect* as an example of the "classic style . . . used to perfection."

Following the death of his daughter Mary in 1930 and in an extreme state of distraction, Pope severely limited his involvement with residential projects and focused most of his attention on obtaining monumental commissions such as the National Archives building in Washington, D.C. But at least one major country house commission, the Laura Delano house (1932), at Evergreen Lands, Rhinebeck, New York, captured his interest due to the prestige of the client, who was his

Fig. 3-78

Fig. 3-79

Figs. 3-79–3-83. The Waves (John Russell Pope house), Newport, Rhode Island, 1928.

Fig. 3-80

Fig. 3-81

Fig. 3-82

Fig. 3-83

mother-in-law and a cousin of Franklin Delano Roosevelt. The house was based on his previous Tudor-style designs, but in this case the plan was extremely compact and carefully arranged. There is a delightful and careful juxtaposition of random ashlar masonry, with half-timbering adding some liveliness to a facade capped by a varied roofline of gable-on-gable and cross gabling. The stone, taken from the ruins of a local church, added to the rusticity of the house and was consistent with Pope's use of such materials for picturesque buildings. It also showed that when Pope focused on a design, he could still produce an excellent and engaging example in a given style.

Although much of the work produced in the last seven years of Pope's career seemed lifeless in comparison with earlier designs, three projects developed in the two years before his death were vigorous and strong, though extremely severe in detail, and thus indicate a newfound vitality.

The first was Dixie Plantation (1936–37) at Quitman, Georgia, which was conceived as a shooting preserve for New Jersey businessman Gerald Livingston. Starting with a massing reminiscent of the Henry White house and a service wing off to one side, Pope adorned the structure with a double-height Ionic portico, a broad frieze band, and a horizontal cornice running across the top of the building, thus uniting the bulk of the house with its slightly recessed wings (fig. 3-84). The rival of any American Greek revival residence, this was his most fluid and coherent work since 1925, and it consequently resuscitated the residential side of his practice.

Pope's final two domestic projects, an unnamed estate by a river and the London residence of Joseph Duveen, continued this promising trend. It is regrettable that these neither of these was built, as Pope seems to have been at his best in these two commissions.

In the first, unnamed project (begun c. 1936), one is confronted with a magisterial edifice of immense proportions fronting on a body of water (fig. 3-85). In this instance, Pope has deftly recast an extensive collection of classical forms, clearly derived from late federal and Greek revival sources, into a reserved ensemble of strength and clarity reminiscent of the work of Robert Mills, who also inspired Pope's monumental work of this period.

Pope continued this approach in the house for his friend, the art dealer Sir Joseph Duveen, Baron of Millbank. For Duveen's London house, near Kensington Palace along the western edge of Hyde Park, Pope began with a carefully proportioned facade based on the square and the golden section, and then developed several decorative schemes based on Greek revival sources. A squarish, pedimented central pavilion served as the background for a series of design experiments for the entrance.

Fig. 3-84. Dixie Plantation (Gerald Livingston house), Quitman, Georgia, 1936–37.

Fig. 3-85. Proposal for an unnamed project (unbuilt), begun c. 1936.

In one proposal, a pilastered pavilion in the Tuscan order enframed a relatively simple entrance topped by a bracketed horizontal cornice (fig. 3-86). The frieze was adorned with laurels, evocative of the Choragic Monument of Thrasyllus in Athens, a favorite source for Pope's monumental buildings. In a second solution, the pedimented central area was adorned with a single-bay Doric porch surrounding the entrance, while a pair of roundels enlivened the second floor (fig. 3-87). The solution for the garden facade (fig. 3-88) was an equally strong classical statement, in which the second floor receded to emphasize the Ionic-pilastered central pavilion and create balconies that softened the general appearance of the facade and eased the visual transition between the house and garden. The project was abandoned on Duveen's death in 1938, just before construction was to begin.

THE CLUBS

Pope was a member of a least a half a dozen private clubs, and that he did not design one before 1925 was probably because most of them had already built new facilities within the previous twenty years. Pope's experience with country houses gave him the proficiency to design appropriate spaces for entertaining, and quarters for sleeping when required. His design approach in these projects reflected a continued reliance on precedent, his own work, and that of his mentors.

Pope's first club was the University Club for Milwaukee, Wisconsin (1925–26), on a dramatic site overlooking Lake Michigan. The most prominent architectural device of the Georgian exterior (fig. 3-89) is the sequence of four delicate pilasters that accentuate the central elements of each facade. Flemish bond brick with variegated coloring give a liveliness to the vast unadorned walls. In the interior, which was detailed in a subdued colonial Georgian, Pope followed the plan he often used in his country houses. On the ground floor, ancillary spaces and a reception hall mediate between the entrance and the living and dining room, which are arranged to take advantage of dramatic views of the lake. As predictable as the facade, the upper floors were devoted to bedrooms for club members, a library, and card rooms, while the basement housed the squash courts and bowling alleys.

Pope's next project, the Tuxedo Club (begun 1927) for the private community of Tuxedo Park, New York, was a pastiche of his standard country house plan, with dogleg additions on both sides forming a picturesque composition (fig. 3-90).

New York's Junior League Club (1927–29), on Seventy-first Street between Second and Third avenues, was a large commission, even for Pope, and the most complex he had handled to date. Not only did the program call for extensive dining and recreational facilities, a glee club, and an auditorium fully equipped with a stage for the theater school, but it also required that an entire floor be devoted to a baby shelter, the League's major charity.

Pope's interior was grounded in well-established precedent: the Georgian revival. The arrangement of the exterior was expressive of the interior organization (fig. 3-91). A point of entrances, one at each end of the building, gives access to the baby shelter and various member services (including a kennel room), and anchored the ends of a slightly projecting central pavilion. The upper floors, originally intended to have a strong setback with a balcony off the baby shelter, were finally conceived as a flush facade with a small balconette.

Pope continued to explore McKim, Mead & White's Colony Club model in the Spence School (1928–30), on East Ninety-first Street in New York. But over the course of a year, the exuberant Georgian-style design (fig. 3-92) was toned down into a more severe solution distinguished by a Tuscan-columned entrance and a vaguely Georgian treatment of the upper floor windows.

In 1929, Pope continued to rely on precedent in his design for the Spouting Rock Beach Club at Newport, Rhode Island (fig. 3-93), which was simply an enlarged version of the Marshall Field bathhouse with some additional colonial revival detailing.

The Marcus Ward Home for Aged and Respectable Bachelors (1924–32, now admitting women to the membership) in Maplewood, New Jersey, was a refuge for older men who had had distinguished careers, but who no longer possessed the ability or means to support themselves. The tone of the facility was somewhere between that of a college dormitory and a men's club. The plan (fig. 3-95) reflected this conceptual organization, with public and private spaces separated and differently articulated. Borrowing from his contemporaneous work at Dartmouth College and Yale University, Pope laid out the complex in a picturesque manner as a series of interconnected structures with courtyards, even though the plan is controlled by strong geometric axes. The dining, medical, and social pavilions were laid out parallel to one another in a staggered sequence, each with a separate service yard. The residential quadrangle was situated at a forty-five-degree angle to the service wings and connected by passageways that created irregularly shaped courtyards. The illusory irregularity of the plan permitted Pope some freedom in the facade design. Because of the lack of apparent connection between the pavilions, details such as eave heights could be varied to meet functional requirements, and a picturesque image was easily achieved. In fact, on approach, the Ward Home seems like one rambling structure,

Figs. 3-86–3-88. Proposals for Sir Joseph Duveen house (unbuilt), London, c. 1937.

Fig. 3-89

Fig. 3-90

Fig. 3-91

Fig. 3-91

when it actually comprises four well-organized pavilions (fig. 3-94). The interiors are consistently finished with Georgian colonial revival detailing, from the sparely decorated sleeping rooms to the larger public rooms, such as the lounge (fig. 3-96), which evokes images of New York's more prestigious men's clubs. Here, Pope created a distinctly American image that evokes a sense of age, dignity, propriety, and permanence—the perfect setting for retired, respectable bachelors.

Fig. 3-92

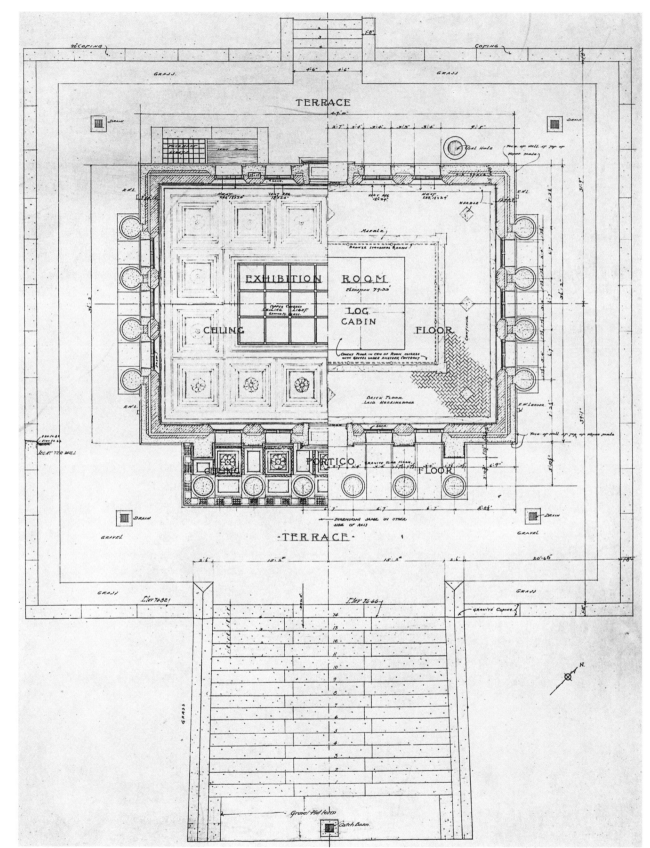

Fig. 4-3. Lincoln Birthplace Museum. Revised plan.

Fig. 4-4. Lincoln Birthplace Museum.

Fig. 4-5. William B. Leeds mausoleum, Woodlawn Cemetery, The Bronx, New York, 1907–09.

Fig. 4-3

Fig. 4-4

Fig. 4-5

a wafer-thin triumphal arch. Although such refined civility was appropriate in a residential setting, it lacked the force and strength that one associates with the legends of Lincoln's pioneer life. It also proved too costly, forcing Pope to reduce his scheme to a structure situated atop a small knoll enshrining only the cabin, with a design (figs. 4-3, 4-4) that immediately evokes images of Leo von Klenze's Walhalla. The sparsely decorated interior was Roman in feeling, with a coffered ceiling whose rosettes were based on those of the Pantheon. The cabin itself was located in the center of the small structure beneath a skylight and behind bronze stanchions. The entire ensemble produced an image that was entirely appropriate to early-twentieth-century conceptions of Lincoln's boyhood.

Pope's facility with the monumental was also displayed in the design of another type of structure characterized by uncomplicated building programs: funerary monuments. The William B. Leeds mausoleum (1907–09, at Woodlawn Cemetery, The Bronx, New York, fig. 4-5) was built for a client who died while Pope was designing his house. As Pope's first major essay in the type, it is a surprising success. Each architectural element is treated as a distinct sculptural element. Set above grade on a plinth whose retaining walls are articulated as a massive scotia moulding, the marble mausoleum relies on its massing, with a stepped pyramidal roof and very few individual elements, for its effect. An emphatic

tension is created between the pilasters *in antis*, which flank the recessed opening, and the corner pilaster strip. The entrance is decorated with various classical funerary motifs. The cornice above the door is derived from the Roman sarcophagus of Cornelius Scipio Barbatus and, like the tripods, was taken directly from the plates of Hector d'Espouy's *Fragments d'architecture antique*, while the overdoor bas-relief depicts two female mourners flanking a Greek stele. The tomb's general form, including the wreath-adorned frieze, is clearly derived from the Choragic Monument of Thrasyllus at the base of the Acropolis. There is also strong similarity between the general parti and Pope's original design for the Lincoln Birthplace Museum, which he was working on at the same time.

The tomb was illustrative of a new sense of restraint in New York's funerary monument designs. Pope was already demonstrating an innate ability to manipulate mass and classical form in such a manner that he created simple, severe forms that elicited an extremely emotional response. Strong and heady words came from the leading architectural critics of the time, who based their assessment on a building whose program was the ultimate in simplicity. Pope was the new star on the horizon, an architect who was developing a properly restrained American classicism.

In Pope's tomb for Peter Fenelon Collier (1910, at Wickatunk, New Jersey), he followed the prevailing mode used in such a rural area: the exedral form, in

which a low stone bench supported by rough dressed masonry flanking an honorific wall created a tight U shape around an altar-like monument whose outline was sculpted in the manner of a Greek stele of the fourth century B.C. The classical aspect is broken only by the bas-reliefs of Celtic crosses acknowledging Collier's ancestral heritage. It is an admirable exercise in the use of architectural form to create a hauntingly contemplative locus. Its reductive nature further demonstrates Pope's ability to manipulate the emotional effect of elemental forms.

Pope would continue to design small, classically derived memorials such as the Lord Memorial Fountain (1910, in Somerville, New Jersey), but it was the larger commissions that brought him more attention. The Temple of the Scottish Rite (1910–16), home of the Supreme Council of the Ancient and Accepted Scottish Rite of Freemasonry, thirty-third, southern jurisdiction, was Pope's first major monumental commission in Washington, D.C., and the one that established his reputation for great skill in the design of monumental buildings.

Pope's involvement with this commission began in 1910. Competition entries were solicited, and he could have been one of the participants and may have submitted a design. However, his initial design has been lost, if it existed at all. At least one of the other invitees was John Carrère of Carrère & Hastings, who was also chairman of the Committee on Professional Practice and Competitions of the New York Chapter of the American Institute of Architects. The AIA had recently enacted strict guidelines for the conduct of competitions, and Carrère alerted the national organization to irregularities associated with the Temple competition, which included the lack of a professional advisor and the Masons' refusal to commit to build the winning design. The AIA declared the competition unprofessional, but in disregard of these admonitions, several architects nonetheless submitted designs that were judged unsatisfactory. In March 1910, "certain architects" were asked to submit further designs, but none of these met the mark either. Then, the Masons' grand commander, James D. Richardson, apparently saw a design by Pope that pleased him. It was probably the design for the Lincoln Birthplace Museum, which had just been published in *Collier's Weekly*. After a series of consultations with Pope, who was not a Mason, a contract was signed in April 1910. Pope then set to work, and initial plans for the site were completed by the end of June, reflecting Commander Richardson's desire to make "the new temple as magnificent as art and money can make it" (quoted in the *Washington Evening Star*, 2 July 1910).

In order to spend an estimated 1.1 million dollars, the budget given for the initial competition, Pope proposed a huge, marble-clad, cubic Ionic temple resting on a massive plinth (figs. 4-6, 4-7). Following the Masonic ideal that a local building should

Fig. 4-8

124 MONUMENTAL ARCHITECTURE 1905–12

Fig. 4-9

Fig. 4-8. Temple of the Scottish Rite. Supreme Council Chamber.

Fig. 4-9. Temple of the Scottish Rite. Atrium.

Fig. 4-10. Temple of the Scottish Rite. Temple Chamber.

Fig. 4-10

125

emulate Solomon's Temple, it was crowned with a gilded dome that was to rise 130 feet above the street. Most of the iconography was based on the numerology of Freemasonry, including the thirty-three Ionic columns, symbolizing the thirty-three degrees of the order, which were to wrap around three sides of the building. Below the column bases and above the entrance, a hypaethral space was to carry a long Masonic inscription. The wings of the plinth were to stretch forward to create an open court for the single entrance, while to the rear it was to curve around to provide sufficient room for a grand staircase and entrance to the upper chamber. Two carved sphinxes, facing one another, were located in the open court. The large plaza in front of the building was terraced with four flights of stairs, each consisting of treads whose number was significant in Masonic terms (3, 5, 7, and 9 respectively, numbers that the Masons associated with Pythagorean mathematics).

Following a prescribed organization, the banquet facilities were to occupy the raised basement. The ground floor was to contain the offices of the grand commander and the secretary general as well as the library, all of which were arranged around a huge atrium (fig. 4-9). The grand staircase leading up to the Supreme Council Chamber followed the curved profile of the rear of the building. A mezzanine level inserted above the ground floor was to contain thirty-three offices for each of the thirty-three active inspectors general of the thirty-third degree for the thirty-three states in the southern jurisdiction. These were laid out in enfilade, in groups of seventeen, with the additional room at one terminus of the suites to be used for the Supreme Council Chamber, furnished in the Egyptian style (fig. 4-8).

The crowning glory was to be the Temple Chamber (fig. 4-10) on the uppermost floor of the building. Consisting of a hollow, seventy-five-foot cube surmounted by a dome pierced with a skylight twenty-five feet in diameter, Pope's design invoked the authority of the precedent of his mentors and the Italian Renaissance. The walls were to be articulated in a decorative scheme that constituted an amalgam of the Pantheon in Rome, McKim's Low Library at Columbia University, and Bramante's Santa Maria delle Grazie in Milan. Large arches, the coffers of which were based on those of the Pantheon, supported the dome, while colonnades supported balconies spanning the space between the piers of the arches. A Bramantesque circular motif decorated the soffits of the arches formed by the outer walls and the semicircular windows placed behind the balconies. The effect of this amalgam was overbearing and overwhelming, lacking any sense of subtlety.

Pope continued to modify the design for another year. Granite and limestone cladding were substituted for the planned marble facing. The building's original size of 225 by 225 feet was reduced to 150 by 181 feet. A low wall was added to the terrace and the two sphinxes symbolizing Power and Wisdom were turned to face outward from the forecourt. The mezzanine was eliminated, and the Supreme Council Chamber was relocated to the rear of the ground floor. The dome was modified to assume a more parabolic shape similar to the dome of Brunelleschi's Santa Maria del Fiore in Florence. The external shape of the dome was expressed as a stepped pyramid, while the intercolumniation was altered at the rear of the building in order to accommodate the thirty-three columns prescribed by the Scottish Rite.

Although the construction documents had been sent to contractors for bids by December 1910, the design continued to be changed. As late as May 1911, to increase the amount of light and to provide a grander setting for the throne, Pope made several alterations to the fenestration and the number of columns in the Temple Chamber. He reduced the colonnades to *distyle in antis*. He lowered the windows so that light appeared to emanate from the rear of the throne and through false doors behind the columns on the side walls. This change made the daylight appear to serve some mystical purpose reminiscent of the light symbolism of the pseudo-Dionysians. The corresponding change on the exterior allowed Pope to insert a classically correct, uninterrupted, orthostatic course behind the bases of the Ionic colonnade. The basic design of the building now invoked the authority of a single classical precedent—the Mausoleum at Halicarnassus—as depicted in the reconstruction drawings of Prix de Rome winner Louis Bernier.

Individual elements of the building were derived from a variety of ancient sources. The columns of the exterior were copied from the Temple of Athena at Priene, while the cornice was based on that of the Erectheum. The proportions of the Doric columns in the atrium matched those of the Temple of Apollo at Bassae, and the inspiration for the central door came from the Temple of Hercules at Cori.

Despite the change of materials on the exterior, Grand Commander Richardson reiterated the Supreme Council's grandiose intentions that the Temple be the most beautiful Masonic building in the world, and reaffirmed his commitment to spend more than one million dollars on the construction and furnishings. Construction began in earnest on 18 October 1911, and the building was completed on 13 October 1915.

On the interior, extremely exotic colored marbles and woods were used to create a series of dramatic, almost theatrical, monumental spaces. In the design of the interiors and their furnishings, Pope maintained a remarkable consistency with the exterior, each space being endowed with appropriately classical ornament. The basement banqueting hall was Pompeian, the ground floor atrium was dark and powerfully Doric, and the Temple Chamber on the upper floor was luminous and awe-inspiring beneath a Guastavino dome.

Each decorative element was based on an amalgam of classical precedent and the symbolism of Freemasonry. The lighting fixtures were based on ancient candelabra and torchères found in the National Museum in Naples. The supports for a large marble table in the middle of the ground floor atrium were based on those for a Pompeian table, the Scottish Rite eagle having replaced the griffin found on the ancient model. The fixed seating was based on that of the Theater of Dionysus at Athens, and other chairs were based on McKim's classically inspired designs for the libraries at Columbia University.

As one of the largest and most expensive private buildings to be constructed in a decade, the temple became the focus of a great deal of critical attention and it established Pope as one of the best monumental architects of his generation. Pope himself was obviously quite proud of it: he exhibited various aspects of the design in the Annual Exhibition of the Architectural League of New York almost every year between 1913 and 1917.

Pope's striking ability to assimilate an idiom of architectural style would characterize all of his later monumental designs. His innate sense of proportion distinguished his buildings from those of his contemporaries and kept his buildings from becoming mere academically correct, even stiff, caricatures of their ancient models.

Finished in the autumn of 1916, the Temple of the Scottish Rite would be the subject of constant praise for the next twenty years. The January 1916 issue of the London *Architectural Review* noted that "this monumental composition may surely be said to have reached the high-water mark of achievement in that newer interpretation of the Classic style with which modern American architecture is closely identified." In 1917, Pope's peers awarded him the Gold Medal of the Architectural League of New York for the design. French Architect Jacques Gréber in his *L'Architecture aux États-Unis* of 1920 described it as "a monument of remarkable sumptuousness . . . the ensemble is an admirable study of antique architecture, stamped with a powerful dignity" (Vol. 2, 17). In his book *American Architecture* (1928), Fiske Kimball used this building and its "overwhelming simplicity and grandeur" as an example of the triumph of classical form in America. The project also earned Pope a place in the 1928 edition of Sir Banister Fletcher's monumental *History of Architecture on the Comparative Method*, and even the adamant modernist Lewis Mumford agreed that it was an excellent example of its type. In the late 1920s, a jury of Pope's peers selected and published

measured drawings of the Temple as one of the three best public buildings in the United States, ranking it with Bertram Goodhue's Nebraska state capitol (1920–32) in Lincoln and Paul Cret's Pan-American Union (1907–10) in Washington, D.C. A poll of federal government architects in 1932 still ranked it as one of the ten top buildings in America. In his first major public commission, Pope had created a landmark in American architecture. His next project would further solidify his reputation. He was ready to to try to obtain the greatest prize of the year, and possibly of a lifetime: the Lincoln Memorial in Washington, D.C.

Pope's involvement in the plan to build a memorial to Abraham Lincoln was the result of a long and complicated political process. In 1901, the Senate Park and Planning Commission (commonly known as the McMillan Commission) designated the terminus of the Mall, also known as Potomac Park, as the site for a memorial to Lincoln, and for years Senator Shelby Moore Cullom of Illinois tried to pass legislation to erect it, but most of his early efforts died on the Senate floor. With the centennial of Lincoln's birth in 1909, three more bills to this effect were introduced, and although they, too, were unsuccessful, they seemed to confirm a certain agreement on the matter among most members of Congress. Finally, in 1911, renewed efforts on the part of Senator Cullom, now joined with former Speaker of the House of Representatives Joseph G. Cannon, resulted in the passage of a Senate bill creating a Lincoln Memorial Commission charged with determining the site, planning, and design of a monument to Lincoln in Washington, D.C. This commission consisted of President William Taft, Senators Shelby Cullom, George Wetmore, and Hernando de Soto Money, Representatives Joseph Cannon, Samuel McCall, and James Beauchamp Clark. The bill authorized the commission to engage artists, sculptors, architects, and other workers to create and produce a monument costing no more than two million dollars, at the time the largest appropriation ever granted for a national memorial. However, the matter was ultimately subject to congressional approval.

At their first meeting, President Taft proposed that the Lincoln Memorial Commission avail itself of the services and advice of the National Commission of Fine Arts. A resolution passed in which the Lincoln Memorial Commission asked the Commission of Fine Arts for its opinion on the Potomac Park site and several sites between Union Station and the Capitol, in addition to soliciting any other suggestions the members might have had. The resolution further called on the Commission of Fine Arts to suggest the best methods for selecting the architect and artists for the project. Given that this would be the first time that the newly established Commission

Figs. 4-11, 4-12.
Proposal for Lincoln
Memorial, Meridian
Hill site, Washington,
D.C., 1911–12.

of Fine Arts would be involved in the realization of a specific aspect of the McMillan plan, acquiescence on any issue to the politically powerful Lincoln Memorial Commission would diminish its emerging authority.

While the Commission of Fine Arts deliberated into the summer of 1911, various groups and individuals lobbied publicly and privately to influence the site selection and choice of architect. The only sites that were strong contenders were Capitol Hill, Potomac Park, Meridian Hill on axis with the White House at Sixteenth Street, and the Old Soldiers' Home site on North Capitol Street. In July, the Commission of Fine Arts issued their report supporting the Potomac Park site.

As to the selection of a designer, in light of the AIA's support of limited competitions, the Commission of Fine Arts wavered, suggesting direct selection of an architect, and alternatively, selection by competition. Meanwhile, while all of the official groundwork was being laid, Pope became interested in the project. He had launched his own campaign to secure the commission in January 1911. With the passage of the legislation, he merely redoubled his efforts.

At the Lincoln Memorial Commission's first meeting to discuss the report, they asked the Commission of Fine Arts to recommend an architect for the memorial. After a brief conference amongst themselves and in their own offices, the Commission of Fine Arts selected Henry Bacon. With the official announcement of Bacon's appointment, Pope must have assumed that there was no chance of his obtaining the commission and wrote his friend a congratulatory note. Senator Cannon, who had come to know of Pope's interest and had his own ideas about how the architect and site should be selected, did not intend to give up easily. In lieu of merely accepting the Commission of Fine Arts's report, he proposed the creation of a three-member advisory committee composed of Bacon, Elliott Woods (superintendant

of the Capitol), and Pope, who would be charged to design a memorial on one of the three proposed sites. At the next meeting of the Lincoln Memorial Commission, Cannon marshalled enough support for Pope to ensure that he was employed to make designs for two of the proposed sites, the Old Soldiers' Home and Meridian Hill.

A decisive factor in the Memorial Commission's apparent reversal may have been dissatisfaction over the recommended method for selecting an architect. The fact that there would be no competition had irritated many architects, and Pope's appointment would have assuaged these sentiments by giving the appearance of a competition without there actually having to be one. Consequently, Bacon explored the Potomac Park site and Pope the two others.

Pope clearly realized that he was to function as either a foil to the Commission of Fine Art's plan, a straw man in a dummy competition, or, at best, a dark horse in Bacon's shadow. Obviously highly

conflicted, Pope nonetheless was determined to make the most of this opportunity and proved himself to be an unexpectedly difficult opponent for Bacon and his supporters.

Pope's designs were extremely bold. For Meridian Hill, he built upon the example of his acclaimed Temple of the Scottish Rite and further elaborated that parti (fig. 4-11). The design was based on early Doric temples of Sicily and the Italian peninsula, but departed from this model in that it was dipteral and lacked a cella. Instead of being hidden within, the large statue of a seated Lincoln, who would be depicted deep in thought by sculptor A. A. Weinman, was intended to be visible from a distance as a giant looming shadow (fig. 4-12).

The scheme for the park-like Old Soldiers' Home site was even more grandiose. One approached the monument by way of a huge forecourt—one thousand feet long and six hundred feet wide. At the terminus of the approach, a six-hundred-foot-square platform supported by grassy terraces rose above the trees on the site to reach a height of 225 feet above the Potomac. In the center of the platform, Pope placed the statue of Lincoln (fig. 4-13), surrounded by a circular Doric peristyle 320 feet in diameter topped by an attic.

In February 1912, the Lincoln Memorial Commission settled on the Potomac Park site. One would have assumed that this was the end for Pope, but in fact he had garnered enough support and interest that he was asked to join Bacon in meeting with the commission to discuss the new site. Both architects were directed to prepare new designs or revise their original ones for the Potomac Park site.

Pope was still in the race, but the status of the project had changed in relation to the AIA's policies and official Code of Ethics. Since both architects were now designing a structure for the same site, their relationship was now purely competitive. This required that there be a program, that terms and conditions be set, and that the selection committee have an architect as its professional advisor. However, none of these requirements was actually met.

The fact that the Commission of Fine Arts, which counted several architects among its members, was to act as an advisory jury, seemed to satisfy the AIA. The minutes of the 5 March 1912 meeting of the AIA Executive Committee reflects that the members obligingly resolved that the "terms of the Code be waived in this particular competition." With this annoyance out of the way, and encouraged that he had made it this far, Pope focused most of his attention on the competition. He decided to revise his Old Soldiers' Home design, along with six or eight other quick sketches based on suggestions made at the previous meeting of the Memorial Commission. When the Memorial Commission met in March, Pope and Bacon presented their designs and several alternatives. In his presentation, Pope quickly dismissed his alternative designs. These sketches, rendered in a free and powerful manner, examined virtually every possible monumental form that one might use for such a memorial, from stepped mastaba to open colonnade, each one adorned with a major sculptural element. But all of them were red herrings that Pope was using to illustrate the point that no monument could make the Lincoln statue the dominant element. His principal design was a minor reworking of the Old Soldiers' Home scheme. As depicted in huge drawings, it was a clear demonstration of a man "going for broke," projecting a scheme of megalomaniacal proportions. But even in its excessive scale, there is a sober aura of raw power that has an immediately seductive appeal. The severity of form is also quite refreshing. Pope achieved his image of monumentality with a minimum of decorative elements and no superfluous structural com-

ponents. His use of the circular form had the advantage that its large portico was strong enough to terminate the major axis of the Mall.

When the two architects had presented their proposals, the executive secretary of the Commission of Fine Arts read its report. Given the commission's commitment to Bacon, the treatment of Pope's designs bordered on the unreasonable. On balance, the Commission of Fine Arts merely reiterated its original recommendation and suggested Bacon as the architect of the monument.

Pope was obviously stung by the criticism leveled by the Commission of Fine Arts and set out to rectify the situation. At this point Pope had invested too much of himself in the competition to recognize that, regardless of any efforts he might make, Bacon was virtually guaranteed the commission. Pope no longer saw himself as the straw man and had by this time mistakenly allowed himself to believe that he was a serious contender.

In April he appeared before the Memorial Commission, making a short statement to plead his case. Finally, after hearing Pope's statement, the Memorial Commission voted on the choice of an architect. Of the seven-member commission, only two voted for Pope. The next day's newspapers were dominated by the news of the sinking of the *Titanic*, but the *Washington Evening Star* did announce the Memorial Commission's decision.

Pope did not, however, lose everything in this competition. His designs were stirring enough to create a tremendous interest among the general public, which resulted in a surprising demand for the continued exhibition of the drawings. After expressing some initial reluctance (for unspecified reasons), the Memorial Commission released them for display in 1914, when they appeared in exhibitions sponsored by Architectural League of New York, the Chicago Architectural Club, and London's Royal Academy.

Despite his loss of the commission, Pope clearly had captivated a certain portion of the architectural world. He had given his all in a losing cause. If he had won, it would have signaled a major defeat for the fledgling Commission of Fine Arts. Too many influential architects on the commission had invested too much time to allow a man who was viewed as being essentially in the employ of the loyal opposition to win and possibly undermine the power of the Commission of Fine Arts. Pope's staying power may have upset the timetable for the monument, but the outcome was never in doubt. Nevertheless, even if Pope had produced nothing after 1912, his place in the history of American architecture would have been secured by his designs for the Lincoln Memorial and the Temple of the Scottish Rite.

*Fig. 4-13. Proposal
for Lincoln Memorial,
Old Soldiers' Home
site, Washington,
D.C., 1911–12.*

CHAPTER 5

PUBLIC BUILDINGS

Pope wanted to become a complete architect in the Beaux-Arts sense, designing buildings that could become the monuments of their communities. His early successes in this area led to a series of increasingly prestigious projects that occupied him until the year before his death.

In 1916 there was much of this type of work to be found in an era of general economic expansion and governmental growth. Winning the competition for the Cleveland Public Library in that year would have been quite a plum for Pope. This was slated to be the fourth building in a plan laid out for Cleveland's civic center in 1903 by Daniel Burnham, Arnold Brunner, and Carrère & Hastings. As one of the earliest and one of the few programs of the City Beautiful movement actually to be constructed in America, the Group Plan, as it came to be known, influenced the development of other cities such as Kansas City and San Francisco. Pope's participation in building for the plan would have signaled his equality with its makers, and perhaps might have led to other commissions elsewhere.

Located at the head of a six-hundred-foot mall, the library was to be adjacent to the Federal Building completed by Brunner in 1911, and the two were meant to relate to one another. The program called for a highly compartmentalized yet comprehensive library to include large public reading areas with open stacks, and separate rooms for reference, music, children's literature, art, science and technology, periodicals, newspapers, folklore, sociology, and patents collections. There were also to be classrooms, a large adminstrative department, exhibition space, and closed stacks for over one million volumes.

Three local architects and eight other architects were asked to compete. Pope was by now wary of unapproved competitions, having already run afoul of the AIA and its guidelines. He gained entrance to the competition, but that did not guarantee his success. In developing his parti, he again turned to a tried and true McKim formula. With the exception of a reading room in a skylit courtyard, in plan and organization his design was based on McKim's

Boston Public Library (1887), although Pope was to give it a more three-dimensional treatment. The planning (fig. 5-1) is very intelligent and logical, but regardless of its clarity, Pope's design was too discordant in relation to Brunner's Federal Building to win. Pope's design used trabeated openings where Brunner had used arches, and arches where Brunner had used trabeated openings. Pope also treated his corners as part of a continuous facade, while Brunner treated them as projecting pavilions. Pope's strong emphasis on mural texture is typical of his work of this period, but the contrast with Brunner's Federal Building facade might have been interpreted as a "correction" to the other architect's work. In addition, a xenophobic reaction was afoot in Cleveland against the Group Plan: it was viewed by locals as a scheme generated by outsiders. After a review by separate juries in New York and Cleveland, Pope placed second to the Cleveland firm of Walker and Weeks, who had submitted designs with facades that virtually matched Brunner's.

In 1915, Pope entered the Newark Memorial competition for a building celebrating the 250th anniversary of the founding of the New Jersey city (fig. 5-2). The program included theaters, a museum, and a school. With the plan's biaxially symmetrical arrangement around open courts (fig. 5-3), Pope attempted innovations that no doubt contributed to his losing the competition. He wrapped the school around the outside of the museum, and although this was a solution that satisfied the physical needs of the program, it would have created an administrative and logistical nightmare. Pope's design was promoted to the final round, where he lost the commission to McKim, Mead & White.

In Pope's next major public building, a city hall (completed 1920) for Plattsburgh, New York (figs. 5-4, 5-5), there is a paradigmatic shift insofar as he apparently abandoned Rome and McKim as direct models, and instead turned to the Greek Revival architecture of Robert Mills and his contemporaries. Pope no doubt saw the opportunity to create an appropriate background for his not yet completed Macdonough Memorial (see Chapter 10),

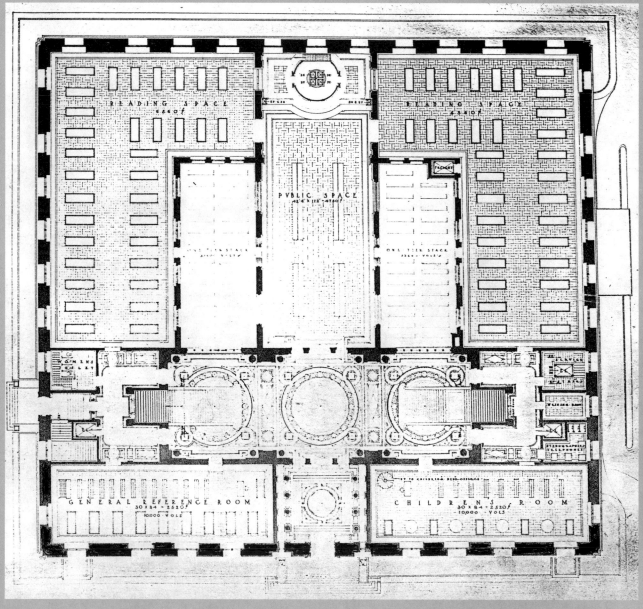

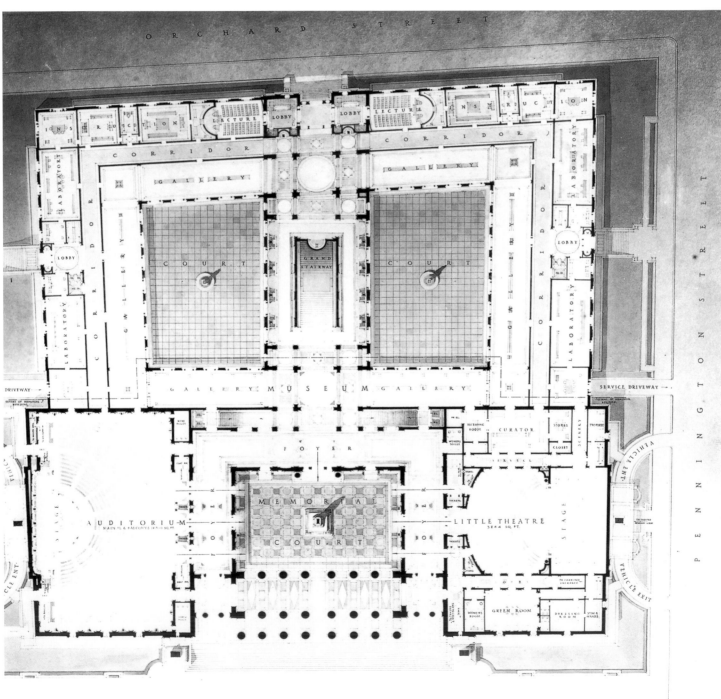

also for Plattsburgh. The city hall commission originated when a local resident bequeathed the funds for the building. Already at work on the Macdonough Memorial, Pope prepared a tentative scheme and was hired in June 1916 as the architect of the city hall.

As completed, the building's two-story plan is quite simple, with all the standard ceremonial rooms such as the court, council chambers, and mayor's office on the main floor. On the second floor, in response to local demands for a large auditorium, Pope designed a large room surrounded by offices. The interior decoration was as spare as the exterior, being reduced to columns with capitals based on those on the Temple of the Winds in Athens.

Despite the praise it received in the press, the building's severity did not draw any followers. But in terms of Pope's work, it marks his first step away from better known precedents, replacing them with American interpretations of classical forms that were appropriate to Plattsburgh's moment of fame—the period of the War of 1812.

With the approach of World War I, the construction industry saw a general slowdown, and public building nearly ceased altogether. But in late 1917, Pope was appointed to the National Commission of Fine Arts, signifying a judgment by his peers that he was a competent designer and critic of public buildings and monuments, and capable of ensuring that the further development of the capital would be in accord with the McMillan plan and that government buildings outside Washington would meet a high standard of design.

At Pope's first meeting as a member of the Commission of Fine Arts on 13 October 1917, the group addressed the form to which future public buildings in Washington should adhere. As an adjunct to this discussion, Franklin D. Roosevelt, then assistant secretary of the navy, spoke to Commission of Fine Arts chairman Charles Moore of his desire to make the opulent Second Empire exterior of the State, War and Navy Building adjacent to the White House (now known as the Executive Office Building, designed by Alfred B. Mullett, 1871–75) conform stylistically to its neighbors and to the Treasury Building. Moore asked Pope to make a few sketches to this end, and he dashed off one that showed a building denuded of its mansard roofs and wrapped in an exterior decoration scheme that mimicked that of the Treasury Building (fig. 5-6). Moore conveyed the sketch to Roosevelt, who was delighted with it and replied, "I need not tell you that I am much interested in the sketch of Mr. Pope. It has always been a pet plan of mine to get this building to conform to the general scheme of the White House and the Treasury. If the Fine Arts Commission can accomplish this, it will have raised a monument to itself for all time." Regrettably, a lack of funds prevented further action. However, in 1928, when Andrew W.

Mellon, then secretary of the treasury, was reconsidering the issue, Moore forwarded to him Pope's drawings in a move that may have helped to influence Mellon's later selection of Pope to design the National Archives as well as the National Gallery.

In 1921, Pope was appointed vice-chairman of the Commission of Fine Arts, but at the end of his term in October 1922, for reasons that remain unclear, President Harding did not renew his appointment. However, while Pope served on the Commission, his fame as a designer of monumental public buildings continued to gain him invitations to important competitions, including one for the Nebraska state capitol. Not only did the invitation signal that Pope was accepted in the realm of monumental public architecture, but his design for Omaha provides further insight into his exploration of the symbols of American classicism.

Under the supervision of AIA president Thomas Kimball of Omaha, a two-stage competition was developed. The initial phase was open only to Nebraska architects, of which three were selected to participate in the second stage against seven competitors from around the country, one of whom was Pope. The structure was intended to accommodate the House of Representatives and Senate chamber with their attendant functions and the Supreme Court and state law library, all in a four-block-square area. Despite Kimball's suggestion to explore new forms, Pope held to established tradition, with an exterior (fig. 5-7) barely deviating from that of the U.S. Capitol. However, Pope used the site and the program to generate a novel and rational plan in which the urban grid generates a biaxially symmetrical plan (fig. 5-8); major paths of circulation within the complex follow the paths of the roads that crossed the site. The quadripartite parti was ideally adapted to the program, allowing separate wings for the legislative and judicial branches. On one side, the Senate chamber and House of Representatives were situated across from one another, separated by a vast hall. On the other side, Pope established a similar relationship between the Supreme Court chamber and the law library.

The exterior, although seemingly traditional in form, is a version of the national paradigm corrected to a more Roman image. The dome is an archaeologically accurate rendition of the dome of St. Peter's; the main portico seems to be based on the Temple of Mars Ultor; some of the frieze decoration comes from the Temple of the Sun and the exterior aediculae from those of the interior altars of the Pantheon.

Pope's classically elegant solution came close to winning. He placed second to Bertram Goodhue, primarily because the jury doubted that his solution could be realized with the given budget. But with Goodhue's dramatic solution, the jury, which was looking for a design that abandoned established

Fig. 5-2. Proposal for Newark Memorial Building, Newark, New Jersey, 1915. Elevation.

Fig. 5-3. Proposal for Newark Memorial Building. Plan.

Figs. 5-4, 5-5. City Hall, Plattsburgh, New York, 1916–20

Fig. 5-6

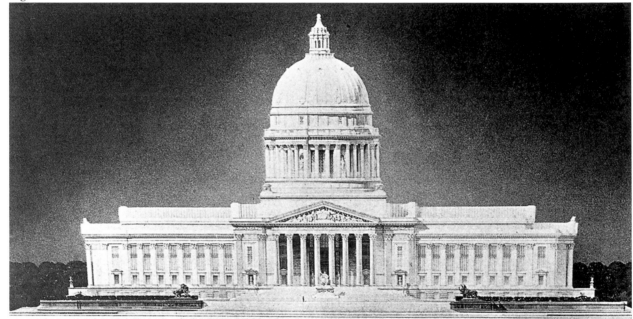

Fig. 5-6. Sketch for remodeling of State, War and Navy Building (unbuilt), Washington, D.C., 1917.

Fig. 5-7. Proposal for Nebraska state capitol (unbuilt), Omaha, Nebraska, 1919.

Fig. 5-8. Proposal for Nebraska state capitol (unbuilt). Plan.

Fig. 5-7

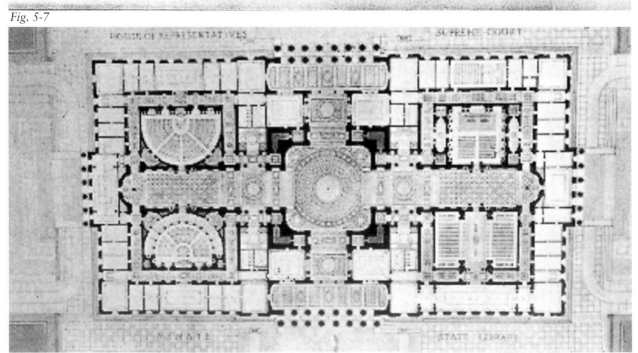

Fig. 5-8

Fig. 5-9

models, could hardly have chosen otherwise. The value of Pope's design lies in the insight it gives into his development. To paraphrase McKim, he had perceived the scale of the project as Roman and worked to fully realize that image. This "Romanization" of form would be characteristic of most of his public commissions, and even in the project for a simple Masonic Temple in Toledo, Ohio (1924), Pope used the entry to the Villa Medici as the parti (fig. 5-9).

It was in the commission for the Constitution Hall of the Daughters of the American Revolution (completed in 1932) in Washington, D.C., that Pope's Roman tendencies become fully manifest. This severely grand structure relies entirely on Roman precedent to hold its place in a very important part of Washington, on Seventeenth Street just south of the White House, facing the lower end of the Ellipse.

In the 1920s, the membership of the Daughters of the American Revolution (DAR) had grown so large that it was difficult to find a location in Washington that could accommodate the thousands of delegates who convened for their annual meetings in April. President General Mrs. Anthony Wayne Cook went to Charles Moore for advice on the selection of an architect, and he asked his fellow Commission of Fine Arts members for advice. Pope was among those suggested, and given that his former client

Mrs. Frelinghuysen was on the building committee, he was selected.

Understanding that the building committee had no clear idea for the auditorium, Pope developed a number of designs during 1924. The program specified a library, a small museum, an auditorium, and vast banqueting facilities. However, Pope's schemes proved too grand for the DAR, so in early 1925 he presented three designs that reduced the size of the auditorium, effected minor changes in the location of the library and committee rooms, and eliminated the museum altogether. Pope continued to work on the scheme that was presented at the annual convention in April 1925 to the entire body of delegates. But this grand design would gradually fall victim to cost-cutting and interminable indecision on the part of the building committee, which resulted in incessant changes to the design. The final design was not approved until April 1928.

As the project proceeded to working drawings, the building committee continue to modify the program, and finally, in August 1928, the members decided to economize even further. While the auditorium retained all of its Roman trappings (fig. 5-10), the facades now became vast expanses of blank wall, which Pope deftly relieved with simple recessed panels and the cogent application of a simple but prominent cornice (fig. 5-11). When the building finally

Fig. 5-9. Proposal for Masonic Temple (unbuilt), Toledo, Ohio, 1924.

opened in 1932, there was scarcely any critical interest in the design, which was by then considered retardataire. However, even though Pope's grandiose plans had been struck down by budget limitations, he had created a building of appropriate Roman grandeur that further dignified and decorated official Washington.

Pope's use of Roman forms continued throughout the 1920s. Using Constitution Hall as his starting point for a parti, and continuing to draw on Roman precedents, he created another example of monumental severity in his Temple of the Scottish Rite (1928) at Baltimore. His simple plan, with ancillary spaces and entrances wrapped around a simple block-like auditorium, was by now a favorite starting point. The source for decoration was the Pantheon, as seen in the main entrance and the window surrounds. A dynamic balance is struck between the highly sculptural window and entrance decorations and the large expanse of blank wall.

In many ways, the American Pharmaceutical Association headquarters building (1928–33) on the north side of the Mall in Washington can be seen as a telling exemplar of the state of Pope's work on the eve of the 1930s. All of his projects tended to reflect straightforward and simple Beaux-Arts planning principles, but the actual forms were validated by both European and American precedent. Designed as one of five buildings that served as backdrops for the Lincoln Memorial, this building is a masterful demonstration of the power of proportion and understatement.

As early as 1912, the Pharmaceutical Association was looking for a Washington site for their headquarters, but it was not until February 1928 that the organization purchased three of the five lots between Twenty-second and Twenty-third streets facing the Mall on B Street (now Constitution Avenue). They had picked a sensitive site for the building. Since 1926, the Commission of Fine Arts had established in principle that B Street would become a monumental avenue running from the Capitol westward to the Potomac. In late 1928, sensing an interesting commission, Pope wrote to William Dunning, the Baltimore pharmacist in charge of the project. His intent was to solicit work, and he got the job.

When the initial design (fig. 5-12), essentially a reworking of Pope's Lincoln Birthplace Museum design, was presented to the Commission of Fine Arts in January 1929, the members clearly sensed that it was cramped by the small site and that subsequent buildings on the adjacent lots would compromise the image Pope had created. Charles Moore wrote to Dunning that the design was approved and that "the Commission of Fine Arts have been solicitous as to a building at this location which would be a portion of the frame of the Lincoln Memorial."

The building was to be a museum, library, and lecture hall, and would include a small research center. But more importantly, it was to serve as headquarters for the Pharmaceutical Association and provide a symbolically prominent place—in the shadow of the Lincoln Memorial—from which the drug

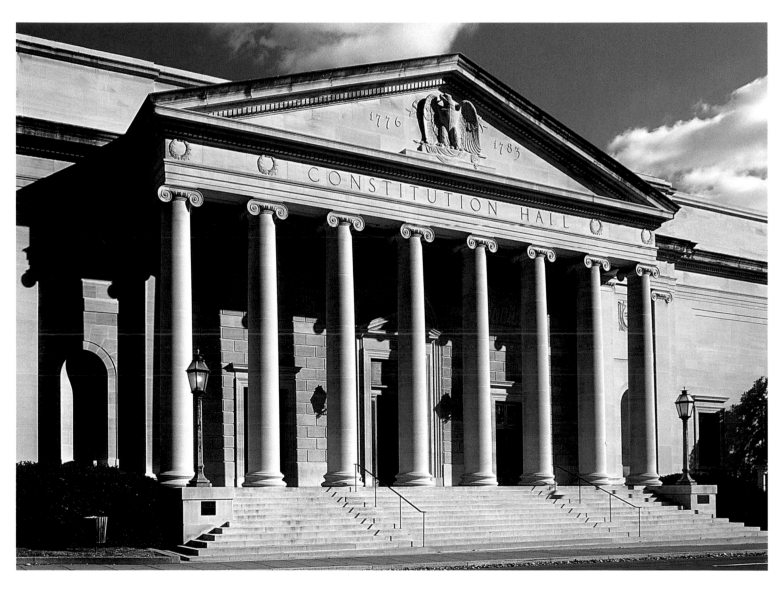

Figs. 5-10, 5-11.
Constitution Hall,
Washington, D.C.,
1924–32.

Fig. 5-12. American
Pharmaceutical
Association Building,
Washington, D.C.,
1928–33.

Fig. 5-13. American
Pharmaceutical
Association Building.
Plan.

Fig. 5-12

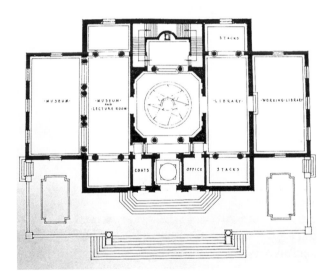

Fig. 5-13

industry could lobby Congress. The plan (fig. 5-13) was extremely simple: a central domed space flanked by large lecture halls or library spaces. To the rear was a deep rectangular recess with a niche for a statue of William Proctor Jr., the founder of American pharmacy (figs. 5-14, 5-16). This domical space, with skylights and ornate pendentives, was decorated in a manner similar to Pope's later Tate Gallery rotunda in London and his Resthaven Mausoleum. The facade was enlivened by a heavy cornice, a stylized triumphal-arch entrance, and vertical alignment of the mortar joints of alternating courses of stone. The same courses alternated in height, creating a sense of texture and tone in the monochromatic surface. By January 1930, the design was virtually complete and Pope was ready to prepare working drawings, but the issue of the site remained unsettled and was not resolved until February 1931,

when the Pharmaceutical Association finally closed on the last piece of property.

The building is one of Pope's best works, an essay in quietly severe monumentality (fig. 5-15). The design is a conscious reworking of the project for the Lincoln Birthplace Museum, and here, in the shadow of Lincoln's effigy, Pope could now present at least one of his aborted memorials to the former president in a location much more visible than Hodgenville, Kentucky. In fact, the only major elements that define the building's relation to pharmacy are the inscriptions and the allegorical bas-reliefs depicting the progress of pharmacy.

In general, the building's decorative elements are flattened, and its monumentality comes from the severity of its form. Careful surface treatments, such as rough dressed masonry surrounding the pilasters, ensure that the austere decorative scheme achieves its greatest possible effect. This technique provides a matte background that mediates between the shimmering marble mass of the wall and the restrained ornamentation. The white marble not only matches that of the surrounding structures, but enhances the appearance of Pope's building and aids in establishing its autonomy in relation to its larger neighbor, the National Academy of Science. The carefully planned setting proved to have been well worth the wait, for it ensured that this jewel-like building would have enough room to breathe.

It is the National Archives and the Federal Triangle projects that establish Pope as the architect responsible for the monumental solution to the problem of massive government offices in Washington. As early as 1923, the city had run out of office space to house the government. The ensuing debate over the best way to solve this problem ended in 1926 with the passage of the Public Buildings Act, which called for constructing fifty million dollars worth of office buildings in a slum area bounded by the Mall, Pennsylvania Avenue, and Fifteenth and Sixth streets. Secretary of the Treasury Andrew W. Mellon was to be in charge of the design and construction of this vast project, while the Public Buildings Commission, led by Senator Reed Smoot, was to oversee the budget and siting of the buildings.

Mellon and Smoot intended these buildings to be beautiful, monumental edifices that would rival those of any other world capital. To ensure this, Mellon appointed Edward H. Bennett to collaborate with the Office of the Supervising Architect of the Treasury, the Public Buildings Commission, the National Capital Park and Planning Commission, and the National Commission of Fine Arts in formulating a unified plan for the proposed site, which became known as the Federal Triangle. Bennett presented a plan to the Commission of Fine Arts in December 1926. The members reacted with disappointment, writing Mellon that they preferred an approach similar to that of the Louvre–Tuileries complex in Paris, with its extensive use of colonnades, open courts, arched driveways, and extended facades along the major avenues.

Charles Moore clearly felt that Bennett was not up to solving the problem by himself. Finally, after meeting with various representatives, Assistant Secretary of the Treasury Charles Dewey recommended to Mellon that a Board of Architectural Consultants be formed to design the complex and suggested inviting Louis Ayres, Milton Medary, William Adams Delano, Arthur Brown, and John Russell Pope. Mellon invited them all, and all of them accepted—with the exception of Pope, who apparently did not reply. He was in Europe and may have replied to Mellon that he would be available as soon as he returned. No one seemed concerned with Pope's apparent lack of response. At the early meet-

ings of the Board of Architectural Consultants, buildings were assigned and a plan was slowly developed. The issue of Pope's involvement was raised in July 1927, but it does not seem to have been pursued, and it is possible that he was the object of some sort of subterfuge among members. Over the next two years, as the Board developed its plans for other Triangle buildings, Louis Ayres's Commerce Building rose along Fifteenth Street, and the Internal Revenue Service building by Louis Simon (head of the Office of the Supervising Architect of the Treasury) was built on Constitution Avenue between Tenth and Twelfth streets.

At the invitation of Charles Moore, Pope attended a meeting of the Commission of Fine Arts in February 1928, where the Board's work was reviewed, but again there was no discussion of his involvement. The National Archives, which had initially been seen as an addendum to the work of the Office of the Supervising Architect, remained to be assigned. By July 1928, various Board members had produced unsuccessful studies for the building, and

Fig. 5-14. American Pharmaceutical Association Building. Initial sketch of interior.

Fig. 5-14

Fig. 5-15. American
Pharmaceutical
Association Building.
Entrance facade.

Fig. 5-16. American
Pharmaceutical
Association Building.
Statue of William
Proctor Jr., founder
of American
pharmacy.

discussion arose about recommending that Pope be retained to advise the Office of the Supervising Architect in its design.

Pope was proposed by Charles Moore, who had been personally involved with the problem of a building for the archives as a result of his membership on the archives committee of the American Historical Association and also as chief of the manuscript division of the Library of Congress. Moore felt that Louis Simon's architects lacked the ability to create an appropriately monumental building, while Pope's ability in this area had been more than adequately demonstrated. The subsequent recommendation that he be hired was clearly the result of Moore's lobbying. Moore sent a telegram to Pope confirming that he would be recommended to design the Archives building. Pope replied that he had been informed that the Board had formally recommended him for the National Archives and that he would be called upon in connection with the Federal Triangle as well. He further indicated his relief at obtaining the commission, as well as having escaped what amounted to blackballing due to professional jealousies. Pope, however, still seemed to present some sort of threat to other members of the Board, and he was not awarded any work for almost a year. His eventual employment stemmed from the Commission of Fine Arts' complete dissatisfaction with the general plan of the Federal Triangle.

For two years the Board of Architectural Consultants had refused to consult formally with the Commission of Fine Arts. Finally, on 25 April 1929, a large model of the Federal Triangle plan was unveiled at a formal reception. The plan had monumental facades facing both Pennsylvania Avenue and Constitution Avenue. The interior of the vast complex was to be filled with open courtyards and passageways. The cross-axis of the Mall at Eighth Street was to be marked by the semicircular profile of the Justice Department building. Between Ninth and Tenth streets, the mass of the National Archives building broke the uniform cornice of the complex, but was surrounded by other governmental offices. Further to the west, between Tenth and Twelfth streets, the Internal Revenue Service building included a hemicycle facing Twelfth Street, which matched a corresponding hemicycle in Delano's Post Office Department building across the street, forming a giant circle larger than the Place Vendôme in Paris. Delano's building and Arthur Brown's Labor and Interstate Commerce buildings required the demolition of the District of Columbia building to form a structure that wrapped around a large internal plaza, known as the Great Plaza (fig. 5-17), which in turn opened onto Fourteenth Street and the Commerce building.

The Commission of Fine Arts was not pleased with the Federal Triangle model and generally condemned it. Commission member and architect Benjamin Wistar Morris commented on its lack of cohesiveness, its appearance of having been designed by committee. Laying strong criticism on the Justice Department building and the facade of the Labor Department building, the Commission of Fine Arts realized that it would have to supervise future progress very closely, and suggested that the model be entrusted to a competent architect like Pope. However, the Commission of Fine Arts could not act officially until the model had been presented to the members, and when it was, they leveled heavy criticism on certain features. They immediately approved Delano's Post Office building and Brown's plans for the Labor and Interstate Commerce buildings, but called for the reevaluation of the central motifs of the Great Plaza. Although they generally approved of Medary's Justice building, they called for the Pennsylvania Avenue facades to be reexamined. The Archives building was generally disliked, and it was specifically recommended that Pope be called in as architectural advisor.

At a Board meeting in September 1929, it was recommended that Pope be added as a member, and he promptly accepted. Since he was appointed at the insistence of the Commission of Fine Arts, he had authority over the other Board members, and he did not lose any time in exerting his influence. At his first Board meeting, he began to take his colleagues to task for the design of the National Archives and the buildings surrounding it. Initially accepting its location between Eighth and Tenth streets, he suggested that the Pennsylvania Avenue frontage be analyzed "to determine if any improvement would result from having the enveloping building of the Archives formed as a more integral part of the main building to relieve the tendency of monotony occurring in the long Pennsylvania Avenue facade." This essentially meant Simon's office would have to start over. The next day, Pope continued suggesting rearrangements, most notably the elimination of the central motif of the Justice Department building, which Medary's partner, Clarence Zantzinger, accepted. Although he could not settle any issue relating to the Archives building, Pope also put forward the use of the Apex building to house the Commission of Fine Arts, the National Capital Park and Planning Commission, and the Public Buildings Commission, and pushed for moving the War and Navy departments to the southeast triangle below the Mall, so that the northern triangle would have a symmetrical counterpart.

Most of Pope's efforts as a member of the Board, however, were aimed at focusing attention on problems in the Federal Triangle plan that had been pointed out by the Commission of Fine Arts. He pushed the Board to develop an acceptable terminus

Fig. 5-17. Model of Federal Triangle plan showing the Great Plaza, 1929.

Fig. 5-18. National Archives, Washington, D.C., 1930–33. Rendering of final scheme.

to the Great Plaza and to see that the pediment of the Labor building conformed to the specifications of the Commission of Fine Arts, and he later gladly reshaped his own Oscar Strauss Memorial Fountain project (1931–37) to conform with the Commission of Fine Arts' demands.

In the context of this focus on the Federal Triangle model, Pope continued to push for an improved design for the Archives building. In January 1930, he proposed that the Pennsylvania Avenue facade be broken at the Archives to form a small square in front of the building. The following month, he presented his most radical schemes for the Triangle, along with a typically short report accompanied by three renderings depicting three serious alternatives for the National Archives. The first two of these, however, were foils to the third design.

The first scheme (fig. 5-19) was simply an expression of the ten-million cubic feet of volume necessary to house the national archives. The second scheme (fig. 5-20) was a response to an earlier suggestion that a forecourt be created for the building, but Pope pointed out that it was in the wrong place and would only be desirable at the terminus of the cross-axis of the Mall. With these two drawings, Pope used the Board's suggestions to establish the proper siting of the Archives building. In Pope's view, the building, due to its special character as the repository of the nation's written history, required a monumental treatment, which was incompatible with the given location and detrimental to the character of the Justice Department building, whose form was to pay homage to the cross-axis of the Mall.

As his own solution, Pope offered the third scheme (fig. 5-21), in which he suggested moving the Archives building to the cross-axis of the Mall, where its monumental qualities could be set off, and moving Zantziger's already-designed Justice Department building one block west. He returned to his proposal that the Archives building should break the established facade line along Pennsylvania Avenue so that a square could be formed to the north of the building, giving one the sense that the Mall would be carried around the Archives. Set off in this manner, Pope reasoned, the building could be given its appropriate monumental treatment, which he envisioned in the form of a massive stone box whose four sides were decorated with pediments. He justified the location by pointing out that it was the best place to break the standard cornice line and also that it would signal something important in the plan of the city. Furthermore, he reminded his colleagues, the creation of a square north of the building was initially proposed in the L'Enfant plan for Washington.

The initial reaction to Pope's proposal was swift and negative. Delano disliked the plan because it meant that the otherwise uninterrupted line of the Pennsylvania Avenue facade would be broken. Arguments

Figs. 5-19–5-21. Three proposals for National Archives, 1930.

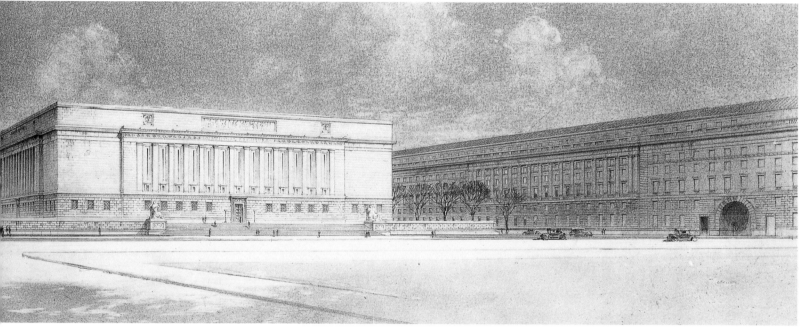

Fig. 5-22. National Archives. Shrine room with Declaration of Independence.

Fig. 5-23. National Archives. Reading room.

Figs. 5-27, 5-28.
National Archives.
Pediment.

Department had been trying since 1927 to plan a new building to house all of the London embassy's consular functions and to provide lodgings for foreign service officers. The State Department had entered into negotiations with the American construction firm Hegemann Harris, which, with British financial backing, was to build a chancery and lease it to the United States. In turn, Hegemann Harris had negotiated with developer Charles Pezcenick to build the chancery on a parcel of land on the eastern side of Grosvenor Square for which he held a long-term lease from the Westminster Estate. Pezcenick's English architect presented a series of plans to Keith Merrill, executive assistant to the assistant secretary of state, but after a frustrating series of meetings, Merrill suggested that Pope would be the best choice. An agreement was made whereby Pope would design the exterior, the offices, and the ceremonial rooms, and Rosario Candela, the well-known New York apartment-house architect, would design the living quarters above. The exterior was to be composed of a light colored Portland stone facade with Adamesque decorative elements. Although its cornice line matched those of its neighbors, the square-footage requirements were so great that, in order to accommodate the apartments, a two-story mansard roof would have to top the cornice.

Fig. 5-29. United States Chancery, London, 1934–36.

For an urban area that was dominated by Georgian brick architecture, the light stone exterior in an Adamesque style was not acceptable. The tradition-bound Westminster Estate insisted that the facade be early Georgian brick above the first floor, with fluted Corinthian columns and a modillioned cornice. Pope duly complied. As completed in 1936, the building is not as impressive as it would have been if the earlier design had been chosen. Consequently, it is neither a success nor a triumph, but merely an expedient solution in circumstances where Pope was quickly losing influence.

RELIGIOUS BUILDINGS

Although Pope's first religious design was a memorial chapel to his uncle, religious buildings represented a minor aspect of his practice, and in fact, most of them seem to have been the primary responsibility of his associate Otto Eggers, whose designs would subsequently be approved by Pope. In the first two known designs, the private chapel (1916–18) at Kill Kare and the summer chapel now known as the Church of the Advent (1909) at Westbury on Long Island, Pope (or perhaps Eggers) based the designs on the English country parish church type, a model that had been used in the United States since the 1840s. In their later churches, Pope (or Eggers) usually begin with a colonial revival treatment that would be followed by a series of single-

nave, stripped-down, Gothic revival alternatives of the type popularized by Cram, Ferguson & Goodhue, in which Gothic detailing was kept to a minimum, with the major effect coming from rough dressed ashlar stone. With this formula established, the firm produced a series of virtually indistinguishable churches across the country.

In academic settings, Pope opted for circular or Greek cross plans for his churches, forms which may have been dictated by their important locations in the midst of or adjacent to campuses that he had also planned. The University Baptist Church (1925–28, fig. 5-30) in Baltimore, located directly across from the main entry to The Johns Hopkins University, is a stone version of Howells & Stokes's St. Paul's Chapel at Columbia University (1907). The equilateral form provided both a focal point opposite Pope's proposed auditorium and a grand entrance to the university campus. The Hendricks Chapel (1927–30), built in association with Dwight Baum at Syracuse University, was in fact a realization of Pope's auditorium proposal for the entrance to the Johns Hopkins campus. It is an updated version of Jefferson's Rotunda at the University of Virginia, and reflects the further influence of McKim's Low Library at Columbia University.

In their last project for a church, the National City Christian Church (1928–32, fig. 5-31) in Washington, D.C., Pope and his office pursued their earlier exploration of both Gothic and colonial revival solutions to help the clients reach a decision regarding style. The chosen colonial revival scheme offered an appropriate image for the church's location at Thomas Circle, where the structure is sufficiently classical and self-important for its place in Washington. Pope had created a perfect solution for a church on this site, facing south toward the monumental image of governmental Washington. In the sense of the genius loci, the church is the religious equivalent of Pope's Archives building. The interior is an updated and Romanized version of the colonial type, with narrow, arched side aisles. In the altar area, Pope employed virtually the same treatment as he used in the Hendricks Chapel and Constitution Hall for the DAR. For a sect that emphasized oratory rather than ritual, this almost Anglican layout initially seems inappropriate, but the external appearance is perfect for the location in the capital.

Fig. 5-30. University Baptist Church, Baltimore, Maryland, 1925–28.

Fig. 5-31. National Christian City Church, Washington, D.C., 1928–32.

Fig. 5-31

CHAPTER 6

CAMPUS PLANNING AND COLLEGIATE BUILDINGS

John Russell Pope's service to the stratum of society that commissioned grand town and country houses, monuments, museums, and galleries is also illustrated in his projects for prestigious college and university campuses. With the exception of Hunter College in New York, all were privately endowed institutions, and none were land-grant colleges or state or religious institutions. His first and most important commission came not from a university president or even its board of governors, but from a rich and loyal Yale alumnus, a satisfied residential client of Pope's who had no knowledge of his talent for large-scale, long-range institutional planning.

Pope's involvement with campus planning in general, and at Yale University in particular, comes from his association with Francis Patrick Garvan, for whom Pope designed three houses and a mausoleum, and his friend Payne Whitney, another affluent alumnus. Together these two men supported an extensive land acquisition program in New Haven, Connecticut, for the university, through which Yale purchased additional land adjacent to the original campus. However, Yale lacked an architectural plan, even though the university had engaged a consulting architect as early as 1913. The Yale Corporation, the university's governing body, found that the lack of a clear plan for the physical development of the campus was an impediment to obtaining further endowment, and in February 1917 an Alumni Committee on a Plan for University Development was formed. In early spring of the same year, Garvan approached Pope to determine his interest in the project. Pope was indeed interested, and assented to Garvan's proposal. Garvan then offered to sponsor a plan for the development of the Yale campus.

The campus at New Haven at that time was spread over fourteen square blocks, but it was divided into three distinct sections. The most visually impressive was the old campus on the west side of the Green. Its collegiate Gothic forms, created by Russell Sturgis, Alexander Jackson Davis, and Charles C. Haight, were interrupted only by the

Richardsonian Osborn Hall (1888) by Bruce Price and the Venetian Gothic Street Hall (1866) by Peter B. Wight.

To the northwest of the old campus was a second section that was the least unified of the three. South of the Berkeley Oval (1893–94), designed by J. C. Cady in the Renaissance revival style, was Richard Morris Hunt's Divinity School (1869), designed in a manner sympathetic to the old campus. Further to the north, across Wall Street, were Carrère & Hastings's grandiose classical masses of Woolsey (1900) and Memorial (1900) Halls, which were both out of place in their location.

In the third section of the campus, to the northwest and southwest, were the predominantly Italianate and collegiate Gothic dormitories and laboratories of the Sheffield Scientific School. Although this area contained a few examples of mid-nineteenth-century Italianate architecture, most of the buildings dated from the turn of the century and were towered, buttressed, and dormered structures of Indiana limestone. To the north of the old campus, the Memorial Quadrangle (1920), designed by James Gamble Rogers, was about to rise, replacing an existing ensemble of small buildings.

With this half-finished canvas, Pope set to work on a plan (figs. 6-1–6-3), most of which was completed in 1917, but the final presentation was not made for almost two years. Pope had arranged for the publication of his plan as a limited edition, large folio-sized book, with each plan and illustration reproduced in lithography or steel engraving. Although he had submitted elaborate printed folios for the Lincoln Memorial competition, the Yale publication was far more ambitious. His grandiose gesture toward publication certainly delayed presentation of the project, although the war was no doubt another factor that inhibited progress.

Using noble precedent to describe his solution, Pope invoked both L'Enfant's plan for Washington, D.C., and Jefferson's plan for the University of Virginia, although his plan for Yale owes little to either scheme. The key to the plan, as far as Pope

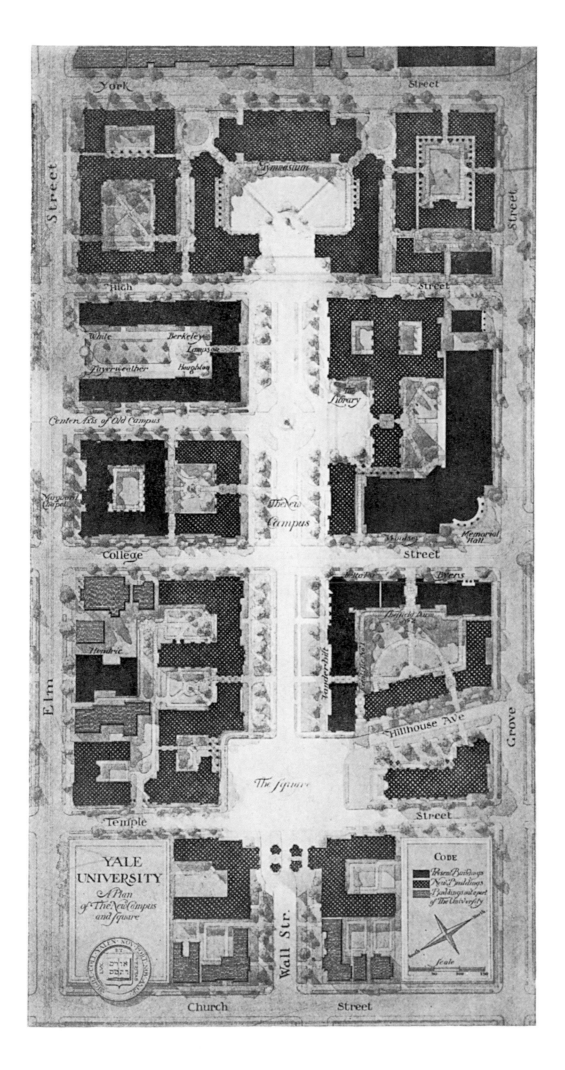

Fig. 6-1. Plan for Yale University, New Haven, Connecticut, 1917–19.

161

YALE UNIVERSITY
A General View of the Proposed Plan

YALE UNIVERSITY
A General View of Existing Conditions

was concerned, was the unification of the campus in order to distinguish the image of the university from that of New Haven. To accomplish this, he had to unite disparate groups of buildings and establish an underlying structure for a new, visually coherent campus. The need to respect the fabric of the city, including its streets and trolley lines, presented further complications.

Pope used standard Beaux-Arts planning techniques, organizing the campus along a series of intersecting axes, with important buildings at the terminus of each axis. He then positioned minor buildings symmetrically along these axes. In his scheme for reorganizing the campus, Pope proposed very little modification to the old campus. He eliminated one building and used the site to create a link to the central section. This move transformed a small street into the major axis, which was to terminate in a new collegiate Gothic library envisioned as the center of academic life. With the main axis delineated, Pope created a new campus on a cross-axis, beginning in the east with a large, open square, and terminating in the west in a massive gymnasium complex. Lining this axis were to be a series of new buildings whose functions, with the exception of the library and gymnasium, were undetermined.

To the north of the old campus a new art school and gallery would occupy one block, while the Memorial Quadrangle would abut the gymnasium. These central portions of the plan created a grandiose entity that was visually distinct from the city and that would certainly have achieved Pope's goals of unity and identity.

To allow for further expansion of the Sheffield Scientific School, a northwest avenue was treated as another axis of the campus, terminating in a grand sciences complex composed of a series of irregularly shaped, open quadrangles that would culminate in a domical observatory.

All of this was to be designed in the English collegiate Gothic style, reinforcing the character of the old campus. Pope advocated the use of a single style, and despite its initial picturesque impression, his was a very controlled version. As in the design of his Gothic houses, picturesque events occurred at symmetrical, predictable, and evenly measured intervals.

Following the established precedent for campus plans, Pope reinforced separate axes to the north and southeast, and thus provided the university with ample space for growth. Creating the second axis made possible a more formal entrance to the campus, and in general gave the university a much greater civic presence. It is a sensible and intelligent plan, guided by a careful study of precedent, and, considering the accepted planning ideals of the day, it must be considered a success.

The compelling renderings by Eggers and their presentation as a printed book added greatly to the

force of the simple plan. The apparent strength and authority of the architecture was derived from direct association with familiar models: the library was certainly influenced by King's College and Great St. Mary's Church, Cambridge, and Magdalen College, Oxford; while the gymnasium and the gateway owed much to Trinity College, Cambridge.

At the next Yale Corporation meeting in November 1919, the Alumni Committee did not comment on the plan, but suggested that three architects act as advisors to consider whether it was necessary for the university to adopt a uniform style; if the plan should be accepted, rejected, or modified; and if the quadrangle system or a more open style of architecture should be used. The Committee asked Cass Gilbert, Bertram Goodhue, and James Gamble Rogers to participate, but ultimately Paul Cret and William Adams Delano replaced Gilbert and Rogers, respectively.

This panel of advisors approved the Pope plan with what were described as several minor changes and two major modifications. Actually, though, their report recommended drastic and substantial revisions. Pope's reaction was one of quiet fury that he had been second-guessed, and the tension between Pope and the advisory panel was so high that, in the case of Delano, it would persist until Pope's death.

As late as December 1920, the decision on the adoption of a general plan was still open. Pope was asked to revise his plan on the condition that he accept the advisory panel's modifications, but he rejected the Committee's terms. However, as late as 1924, the Yale Corporation continued to voice its thanks to Pope when it approved James Gamble Rogers's plan for the university, which carries out most of the key ideas of Pope's plan. Despite his obvious disappointment, Pope accepted subsequent commissions from the Yale Corporation, and received an honorary master's degree from the university in 1924 for his role in the creation of the comprehensive planning scheme for the architectural development of Yale.

In late 1921, just as Pope's work on the Yale plan was ending, he was asked by President Edward M. Hopkins of Dartmouth College to develop a scheme for the enlargement of the campus plan (c. 1907) conceived by Charles A. Rich, who had built most of the buildings on campus since 1890. Pope, probably selected because of his work at Yale, agreed, with the understanding that he would be commissioned to design a new dormitory.

Rich's plan followed the New England village model of grouping buildings around a green, but it provided no focus. Pope solved this problem by adopting an axial scheme similar to those at Yale and the University of Virginia (fig. 6-4). The main axis was to terminate at the north with a new library and

Fig. 6-2. Plan for Yale University, 1919. Rendering of Pope's proposal.

Fig. 6-3. Plan for Yale University, 1919. Rendering of original site.

at the south with a new hotel. To the east and west, open quadrangles were completed, while a cross-axis and a diagonal axis similar to the Yale plan diverged at the northern end of the campus. However, the plan offered no protection from the extreme New Hampshire winters.

Pope maintained unity with the existing Georgian-style campus by designing in the same idiom. He built only one building, Russell Sage Hall dormitory, but it was crucial because it defined the cross-axis of the mall. Ultimately, though, the plan represented little progress.

Given the limited realization of Pope's work at Yale and Dartmouth, it is somewhat surprising that The Johns Hopkins University in Baltimore asked him to add to its master plan in 1924. The original plan, based on Parker Thomas & Rice's winning competition design of 1904, was a biaxially symmetrical composition equal to any Pope had produced. Organized around a cross-axis with a third asymmetrical axis, the campus was begun in the colonial revival style, in homage to Homewood, a federal-style mansion and the ancestral home of the Carroll family, which occupied a prominent position on the site.

Pope was brought in by Francis Garvan, who was a descendant of the Carrolls, and who was inter-

ested in endowing the university with a law school. He may have wanted to ensure that any new building was a noble enough backdrop for his institution. With such a strong existing plan, there was little room for Pope to intervene, but he did grasp that the lawn needed a stronger focus, which he created by proposing a grand, domed auditorium, to be known as University Hall (fig. 6-5). The design was never built and its place was finally taken by the unassuming Eisenhower Library.

Johns Hopkins was not Pope's last campus plan. He collaborated on three others with Dwight James Baum: Syracuse University in Syracuse, New York (1922–29), Hartwick College in Oneonta, New York (1929), and Hunter College in New York City (1927). In designing these campuses Pope repeated his previous method, proposing stylistic unity and axial organization. In each case, a centrally located, domed building is flanked by carefully organized groups of buildings. In the case of Syracuse, he created a focal point with the Hendricks Chapel and an auditorium (fig. 6-6). In the plans for the much smaller Hartwick (fig. 6-7) and Hunter (fig. 6-8) colleges, he used a simple cross-axial plan with a domical focus, a Beaux-Arts-inspired parti that was validated by the formidable historical precedents of Jefferson and of Joseph-Jacques Ramée at Union

College in Schenectady, New York. With the exception of Hunter College, these plans were carried to some degree of completion, with a few undistinguished buildings being designed for each one.

While none of Pope's plans was completed as designed, each demonstrated his ability to project coherent, large-scale ensembles. Each plan is lucid and intelligent, even if strictly conventional. All are guided by careful study of precedent in state-of-the-art campus planning between the beginning of World War I and the rise of modernism.

Pope also participated in the design of individual buildings for several academic institutions. In most of these, his office merely supplied the manpower for a smaller firm's design, as at Syracuse University and Hartwick College. In other, essentially "bread-and-butter" jobs, Eggers and Higgins were in charge of work that was of no interest to Pope. In effect, he was only substantially involved with the buildings for Yale, particularly the Payne Whitney Gymnasium (1926–32); Calhoun College (1929–33); and Silliman College (1932–40), the final shape of which was not formulated until after his death.

In 1923, the Yale Corporation approved a program for the Payne Whitney Gymnasium, and in 1925 decided to appoint Pope as architect and to add the Y Club to the program as the headquarters of the Athletic Association, as well as the site of bowling alleys, meeting rooms, and quarters for visiting teams. Pope's sketches (fig. 6-9) show a Gothic design based on the gym in his original plan for Yale. A stubby, recessed tower was flanked by two long, low masses housing a pool on one side and an "amphitheatre" for basketball and tennis on the other, with other sports requiring less room housed in the basement and the tower. The Y Club extended as a separate building from the southern end of the gym.

President James R. Angell was deeply impressed by Pope's scheme. In 1929, the Yale Corporation authorized construction, provided that the cost not exceed six million dollars, which required Pope to reduce the cubage of the building. While the parti did not change, the general articulation of its component parts did. The flanking pavilions became more square in plan, while the buttressed elevations were stepped back almost in emulation of the nave of a Gothic cathedral. At street level, an arcade relieved the massive walls, and this was echoed as blind arcading on the level above. Flanking the central tower and acting as intermediary elements between the massive side pavilion were two projecting towers with central doors decorated as if they were intended for churches. The central tower became more sculptural and transparent. Corner buttressing rose almost to the top of the crenellated structure, while a multi story Gothic window added

Fig. 6-5. Proposed plan for The Johns Hopkins University (unbuilt), Baltimore, Maryland, 1924.

165

lightness and revealed the massive depth of this central element. The main entrance was interpreted as a cathedral portal, replete with statuary and bas-reliefs representing Yale's sports history. The Y Club, appended via an archway, was reminiscent of an Oxford college.

Completed in 1932, this vast gymnasium occupies 510 feet of street frontage to a depth of 206 feet. Its tower rises two hundred feet above ground, making it one of the largest buildings on campus. The Ray Tompkins House, as the Y Club came to be known, is attached to the gymnasium as if it were an ornate rectory and the gymnasium were a cathedral. Its highly decorative interiors continued the lush effect of Gothic splendor, which, in conjunction with the gym, covered the entire block.

Soon after Pope received the initial commission for the gym, the Yale Corporation addressed the university's housing problem. A long list of ills was brought on by a lack of class cohesiveness; the faculty's loss of a sense of responsibility for the students brought on by large, impersonal lectures, and greater numbers of students in entering classes; increasing freedom of curriculum; the intermingling of upper and lower classmen in residential halls; and increasing disturbance caused by automobiles. In December 1928, the university decided to build four freshman dormitories to form the new campus cross-axis. They were to be organized according to the English example. James Gamble Rogers was to design three of these, while Pope was assigned to do a fourth, Calhoun College, on the site of Richard Morris Hunt's Divinity School, as soon as funds could be found to relocate the latter. The trustees of the estate of John Sterling subsequently provided the funds, and in April 1929 Pope presented plans for the building.

Located on a key spot at the end of the Old Quadrangle and diagonally across from the Green (figs. 6-10, 6-11), Pope's design continued the Gothic form and rhythm of the Price and Sturgis buildings on the Old Quadrangle. The general form and outline could also link it to any of a number of colleges at Oxford or Cambridge, especially Balliol College, Oxford. To further this medieval image of the separation of city and university, a parapet wall and dry "moat" adjacent to the building were to be used to buffer the street noises and provide light to the basement windows. Four arched entries were to open onto a large courtyard. The portion facing the new cross-axis was to house a senior fellows' suite and a large dining hall. Resident fellows' suites were located at the Elm Street (southern) entry.

In 1930, oil baron Edward Harkness gave fifteen million dollars to create a college system at Yale, thus necessitating a change in the plans. Freshmen were now to be housed in the Old Quadrangle, while upperclassmen were to occupy these new colleges.

Fig. 6-6. Proposed plan for Syracuse University (unbuilt), Syracuse, New York, 1922–29.

Fig. 6-7. Proposed plan for Hartwick College (unbuilt), Oneonta, New York, 1929.

Fig. 6-8. Proposed plan for Hunter College (unbuilt), New York, 1927.

Pope drastically reduced access—a wise idea in an urban setting—to two entries, and made other changes, such as relocating the dining room and its adjunct common room, and adding a residence for the master of the house.

The design represented both an extremely forceful image and one that paid homage to the adjacent Old Quadrangle. As completed, it is a sensitive adaptation of the Oxbridge type of residential college, and it provides a much needed sense of continuity to the public face of the Yale campus. This was achieved by Pope's use of rough-seam granite laid in irregular courses with random jointing facing the street-front. On the cross-campus sides of the building, a smoother, lighter stone was used to match that found on adjacent Harkness Hall. In the more intimate Harkness Quadrangle, Pope, seeking a friendlier atmosphere, switched to reddish and buff-toned brick. The interior spaces are excellent adaptations of the Jacobean style. The exception is the master's house, which was designed in Wren-inspired baroque and Georgian styles.

Pope's completed buildings at Yale added to the image of the campus, and by that measure were a success. The gym provides a wall-like terminus to the northwestern end of the campus, while Calhoun College links the old and new campuses and provides part of the Gothic border that defines the Yale campus as it faces the New Haven Green.

Fig. 6-9. Initial proposal for Payne Whitney Gymnasium, Yale University, New Haven, Connecticut, 1926–32.

Figs. 6-10, 6-11. Initial proposal for Calhoun College, Yale University, New Haven, Connecticut, 1929–33. Plan and rendering.

Fig. 6-9

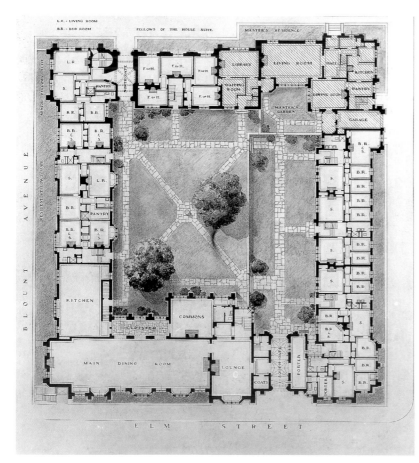

Fig. 6-10

Fig. 6-11

169

CHAPTER 7

MUSEUM BUILDINGS

Fig. 7-1. Baltimore Museum of Art, Baltimore, Maryland, 1925-33.

Fig. 7-2. Baltimore Museum of Art. Plan.

The period from 1870 to 1940, which coincides almost exactly with Pope's lifetime, was the era of greatest museum building in United States history. This period begins with the founding of the Museum of Fine Arts in Boston and the Metropolitan Museum of Art in New York, and ends with the completion of the National Gallery of Art in Washington, D.C. By 1939, at least twenty percent of the world's museums were to be found in the United States, and already by the early twentieth century the American museum had become fairly well defined as a building type.

Despite Pope's initial success with the Lincoln Birthplace Museum, other such commissions eluded him until he won the competition for the Theodore Roosevelt Memorial at the American Museum of Natural History in New York in 1925 (discussed in Chapter Eight). Hard on the heels of that commission, Pope, through the influence of his Baltimore residential patrons the Jacobses and the Fricks, was asked to design a new art museum for Baltimore (fig. 7-1). In plan and general treatment of the building, Pope relied on French precedent. His first concept consisted of a biaxially symmetrical building with a slightly projecting portico that served as the main entrance and principal facade element, denoting a large central hall flanked by rooms arranged around an enclosed central court or gallery. Here, Pope was building on previous experience insofar as his parti was essentially a doubling of the organizational plan employed in his first project for the Lincoln Birthplace Museum. The final floor plan of the original Baltimore Museum of Art (it has been altered several times) was very close to Pope's original sketch (fig. 7-2).

In regard to the general effect of the museum, Pope continued in the vein established for his Roosevelt Memorial and other recent major public building projects such as the Constitution Hall and the Nebraska capitol. However, he borrowed the general external shape of Robert Mills's Patent Office (1836–40), with details adapted from George Hadfield's Old Washington Courthouse of 1820. In place of Hadfield's Ionic order, Pope substituted his own favorite, the Ionic of the Theater of Marcellus in Rome. The portico (fig. 7-3) is based on Pope's Continental Hall, but he improved on that precedent by pushing it forward and flanking it with niches.

The Baltimore Museum of Art set the standard for Pope's future museum designs. An exterior of reserved monumentality is relieved by carefully placed stringcourses, niches, and recessed panels. The limestone masonry is carefully graded in size and tone to create an image of strength and continuous tonality. The same care was employed in the basilica-like central sculpture hall (figs. 7-4, 7-5), whose shape is reminiscent of Lord Burlington's Assembly Rooms in York (1731–32), but whose details are borrowed from the Pantheon and the Theater of Marcellus. More importantly, however, this scheme establishes a formula in which major spaces such as galleries are not clustered together in an unending and overwhelming mass, but are interspersed with large open spaces that add a calm, contemplative feeling to the museum setting.

In anticipation of the gift of the Jacobs collection of Old Master paintings, Pope was asked to enlarge the museum in 1933. He repeated the original building's parti, creating an exterior court behind the sculpture hall and arranging galleries around it. Corner galleries in the addition were to be octagonal, while wings containing an auditorium and administrative spaces were to be separated from the main exhibition spaces by interior courts. But given the Depression-era economy, only the central portion was completed (1937), and that as a Public Works Administration project.

The completion of the initial phase of the Baltimore museum in 1929 marked the beginning of a flood of commissions for Pope, who in the next eight years participated in the design of at least nine museums. In the first year alone, he was asked to make studies for the expansion of New York's Metropolitan Museum of Art and the Cloisters, as well as London's Tate Gallery and the British Museum. What precipitated this wealth of work is unclear,

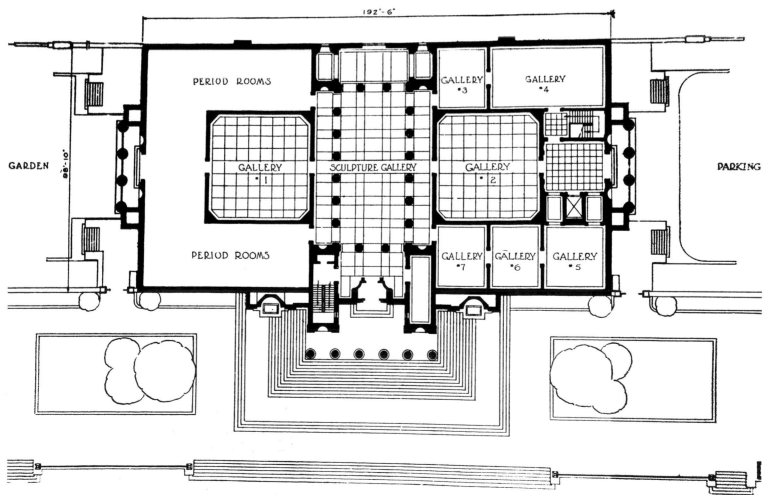

Fig. 7-3. Baltimore
Museum of Art.
Entrance facade.

Fig. 7-4. Baltimore
Museum of Art.
Sculpture gallery.

Fig. 7-5. Baltimore Museum of Art. Sculpture gallery.

but it was probably a philanthropic culmination of the optimism and economic expansiveness of the previous decade.

The scheme for the Metropolitan Museum (fig. 7-6) called for a large new wing to the northwest, and Pope predictably developed an exterior closely matching the adjoining wing designed by McKim. The upper levels were to house the Assyrian collection (fig. 7-7) in spaces that matched the monumentality of the sculpture itself, while an armor court, designed in a late medieval style, was to be embedded at the center of the structure. Pope repeated the courtyard and gallery scheme, which was an arrangement that was becoming a leitmotif of his museum de-

signs. Although this plan was shelved with the advent of the Depression, Pope was later asked to redesign a portion of the existing building (presently the Tapestry Hall) as an armor court—completed posthumously—whose treatment amounted to a diluted variant of his original schemes.

The British were cognizant of the fact that Americans, and Pope in particular, were developing a unique form of classicism. Thus it comes as no surprise that Joseph, first Baron Duveen (1869–1939), connoisseur and English art dealer to many rich American clients, would choose Pope as the architect for the installation of the wing housing the Elgin marbles at the British Museum, as well as the

Figs. 7-6, 7-7. Proposed wing (unbuilt), Metropolitan Museum of Art, New York, 1929.

Figs. 7-8, 7-9.
Modern Sculpture
Wing, Tate Gallery,
London, 1929–37.

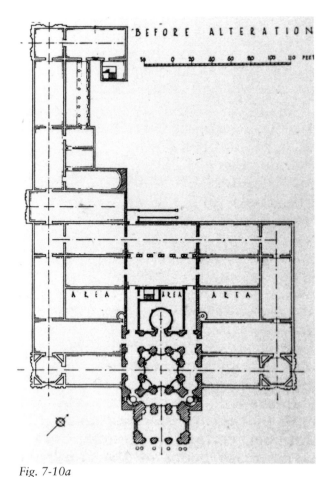

BEFORE ALTERATION

Fig. 7-10a

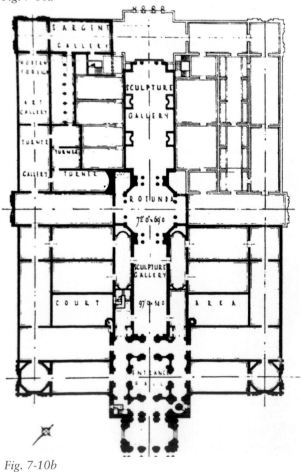

Fig. 7-10b

Figs. 7-10a, 7-10b. Modern Sculpture Wing, Tate Gallery. Plans showing earlier wings (top) and Pope's additions (bottom).

Fig. 7-11. Elgin Marble Wing, British Museum, London, 1930–39.

modern foreign sculpture wing of the Tate Gallery—both of which he proposed to donate to these institutions. Duveen had known Pope since about 1920, and quickly became one of his greatest promoters and friends.

As early as 1927, Duveen had offered the Tate a new gallery to house all of the modern foreign sculpture as a supplement to his and his father's previous donations. But Duveen was later asked instead to fund an entire east wing for the gallery, with offices and storage space above the flood level of the Thames. Since this was not considered an architecturally important part of the building, the British firms of Holden, Adams and Romaine-Walker, Jenkins were proposed to collaborate on the design. Duveen approved the idea, but added that he had little faith in the ability of the architects. It eventually became apparent that he preferred to build the sculpture galleries, not an east wing; that he found any work by the appointed architects unacceptable; and that he would postpone construction until he obtained a design in the latest American style. In 1930 he announced that Pope was designing the wing.

Pope's design was approved by the trustees of the Tate Gallery in 1933. The scheme followed Gaudet's general guidelines concerning apparent sobriety and appropriate lighting; the simple monumentality of the space (figs. 7-8, 7-9) created a daunting backdrop for most of the Tate's collection. The general organization—a pair of side- and top-lit vaulted galleries with a central rotunda and smaller side galleries linking those galleries already donated by Duveen and his father—would seem to have come straight from the writings of Durand. It was an ingenious piece of planning as well, for it provided a focus and symmetrical organization for the earlier wings (figs. 7-10a, 7-10b). And, since it was hidden from view on all sides, Pope focused his efforts on the interior architecture.

The central galleries are based on McKim's designs for the wings of the Metropolitan Museum, while the rotunda is a scaled-down version of Pope's Union Station in Richmond. There is also a strong resemblance to Rafaello Stern's Braccio Nuovo of the Vatican Museum (1806–23). The details are Roman: Ionic columns again based on those in the Theater of Marcellus, and coffered rosettes in the extrados evoking the coffered dome of the Pantheon. Pope was pursuing a standard parti while basing his articulation of the space on the classicism of his predecessor and mentor McKim. But he placed his own imprint on the structure in his use of specific Roman elements and a careful attention to detail.

Using a very few elements to compose and control the space, Pope took great care in the treatment of the stonework. The marble was carefully arranged so that the natural variations of the colors in the stone created an even transition from dark to light. The stone courses decrease in height as they ascend,

Fig. 7-11

Fig. 7-12

Figs. 7-12–7-14.
Proposals for
Elgin Marble Wing,
British Museum.

Fig. 7-13

Fig. 7-14

providing an almost seamless backdrop for sculpture and quietly adding to the design's sense of mass and simplicity. Despite the fact that King George VI called it the "greatest sculpture gallery in the world," the *London Times* of 30 June 1937 described the building as "a striking object lesson in the difference between size and scale," and echoed the general fear that the sculpture would seem dwarfed, blaming the problem on the scale of the Ionic columns. Admittedly, the space was grand and severely monumental, but today the architecture holds its own, co-existing peacefully with the extremely large scale of the late twentieth-century sculpture that is frequently exhibited there. In providing a terminus for the older portion of the building, Pope had sympathetically created a great addition to what Duveen's father had built, and provided a glorious monument to his patron—a key to obtaining more work.

Lord Duveen had offered to build new galleries at the British Museum for the Elgin marbles (figs. 7-11–7-15) and the Nereid monument, and in late 1929, he asked the Trustees to consider drawings by Pope. Duveen, who had already set Pope to work, was on his way to Berlin to study the installation of the Greek and Near Eastern antiquities in the Pergamon Museum. By June 1930, Pope had submitted plans for a wing so immense "it will make the rest of the British Museum a dog house," as Director Sir George Hill was reported to have said. In a large I-shaped hall, the Parthenon frieze was to be incorporated into the walls of the long section, while the pediments were to be freestanding in end rooms reached by a flight of steps flanked by a pair of Doric columns *in antis*, and decorated with the metopes raised on plinths.

The museum's director appointed three professors of ancient art to comment on Pope's design, and thus began a battle that pitted Pope and Duveen against the experts, who believed that the proposed building dominated the sculpture, which they also thought had been assembled misleadingly. They objected to the style of the metope plinths, which made them appear to be steles; the use of a single pedestal base for the pedimental sculpture; and the elaborate paving of the galleries. After five years of negotiation, the building was scaled down by half, the frieze display was pulled forward, away from the wall, and the metope plinths were reduced to simple shelves. The pedimental sculptures were placed on separate bases in relatively accurate positions. The floor decoration was reduced to a Greek key and floral pattern.

Construction began in 1937, and the wing opened without fanfare in 1939, under the cloud of World War II. Although the academic advisors remained disparaging, the gallery's quiet severity and almost overbearing simplicity did function as a unit with the marbles. In his somewhat casual attitude toward

Fig. 7-15. Elgin Marble Wing, British Museum.

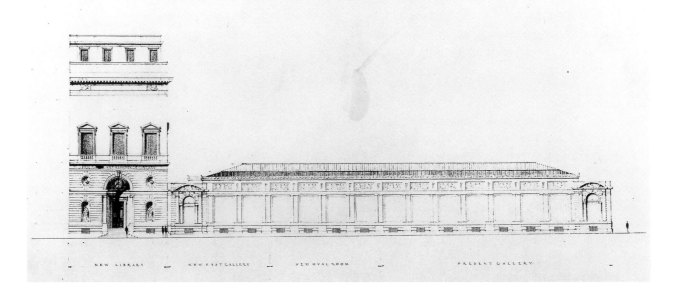

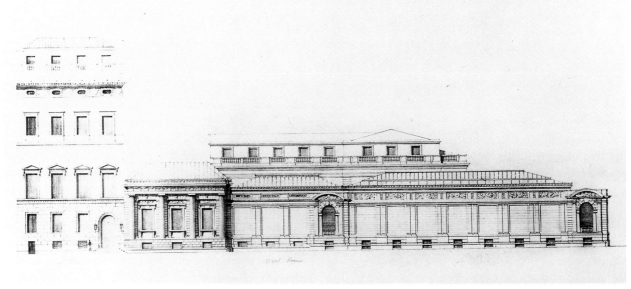

Fig. 7-18. Earlier (top) and later (bottom) rear elevations of Frick Collection (right in drawings) and Art Reference Library of 1933–35(left in drawings), New York.

Fig. 7-19. Frick Collection, New York, begun 1931. Rendering of entrance.

Fig. 7-18

Chicago, but his submission was not what the modernist jury was looking for.

Pope's final museum work, often considered his best, was his commission for the National Gallery of Art in Washington, D.C. (figs. 7-28–7-34). An earlier National Gallery (now known as the National Collection of Fine Arts), a division of the Smithsonian Institution with Andrew Mellon as a member of its oversight committee, had existed. But in 1926, Mellon suggested to the press that a separate national gallery of paintings be established in Washington, and rumors circulated that it would be funded by him. His diary entry for 26 February 1928 actually indicates that he and his family were considering such a gift, but relatively little is heard of this proposal until the time of Mellon's infamous tax trial.

Accused of tax evasion on his 1931 federal return, Mellon took his case to the Board of Tax Appeal. As part of the testimony, his attorneys divulged his gift, which was reported as front page news in the *Washington Post*. Immediately, Charles Moore, who was still chairman of the National Commission of Fine Arts, as well as Pope's close friend, set to work. He initiated correspondence with Mellon, and an interview for this "unofficial project" was arranged for Pope. Who else could be considered if one wanted a classical design? Charles Platt and Cass Gilbert were dead, and Delano & Aldrich were virtually retired from practice. The work of French architect Paul Cret was a bit too modern for a building of such stature. That left only the firms of Arthur Brown (unlikely, due to his location in San Francisco); York and Sawyer (who were known primarily as bank architects); and Zantzinger, Borie & Medary, whom Mellon and Pope had chastised and bullied in the Federal Triangle project. Pope was interviewed in early December 1935, and he immediately set to work. The only other major project in his office at the time was the Jefferson Memorial, so Pope virtually split his staff in two, assigning equal manpower to each project.

Fig. 7-19

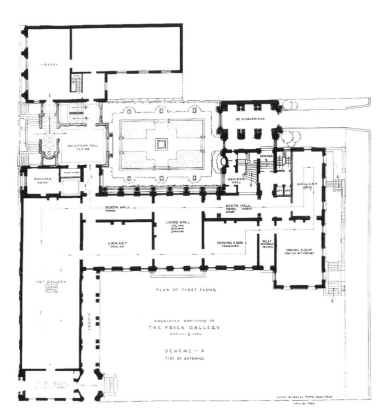

Fig. 7-20

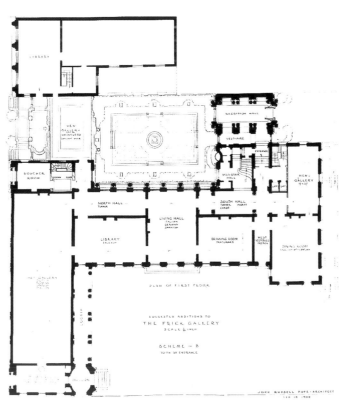

Fig. 7-21

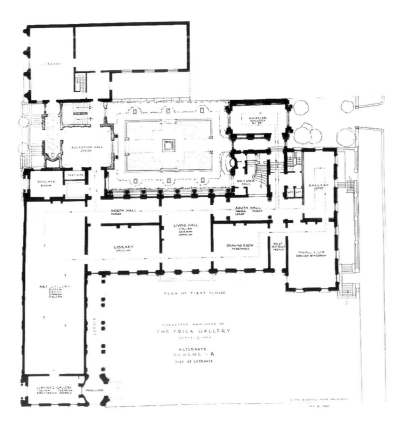

Fig. 7-22

Fig. 7-23

THE FRICK

Fig. 7-20.
Frick Collection.
Plan, ground floor
(scheme A).

Fig. 7-21.
Frick Collection.
Plan, Second floor
(scheme A).

Fig. 7-22.
Frick Collection.
Plan, ground floor
(scheme A alternate).

Fig. 7-23.
Frick Collection.
Plan, ground floor
(scheme B).

Fig. 7-24.
Frick Collection.
Rendering of
garden court.

Fig. 7-25. Frick Collection. Entrance.

Fig. 7-26. Frick Collection. Oval room.

Fig. 7-27. (Opposite) Frick Collection. Garden court.

Fig. 7-25

Fig. 7-26

Fig. 7-29

Now that he had proposed to erect another building that effectively would mask it from the Mall, certain portions of its southern facade were no longer considered crucial, because that facade would be hidden from the Mall.

In order to facilitate Congress' acceptance of the terms of the gift, the Commission of Fine Arts held a meeting at which Moore was authorized to send a letter to Congress endorsing the plans—implying that the general design of the building was approved. Then the commission held a meeting with the National Capital Park and Planning Commission to discuss the closure of Sixth Street, at which NCPCC chairman Frederic Delano said he had talked with Mellon on several occasions about this issue and Mellon had made it clear that unless Sixth Street was closed, there would be no National Gallery built in Washington. With this threat in mind, the NCPPC seemed to acquiesce to Mellon's demands, but at the same time deferred any final action.

The design was released to the press as being approved, which, according to a strict reading of the minutes, it was. President Roosevelt, having seen the plans, took a personal interest in the completion of the project and publicly advised Congress to accept the gift. However, the architects on the Commission of Fine Arts intended only that the site be approved,

and were enraged that their motion was interpreted as a carte blanche approval of the entire project. But theirs were not the only outspoken criticisms of Pope's design. The League for Progress in Architecture, already a thorn in Pope's side since the Jefferson Memorial project, began its attack by damning the classical portico of the building. Obviously Pope was in for a fight, since his friend Charles Moore was not going to be able to control the Commission of Fine Arts, and the younger members were lining up to take their shots at such a large and easy target.

Despite these problems, the enabling legislation was working its way smoothly through Congress. By early 1937, most impediments to the designation of the site had been removed: the George Washington Memorial Society had relinquished its claims, and the citizens' associations had withdrawn their objections to the closure of Sixth Street. In March 1937, the bill passed the House and Roosevelt signed it into law.

The members of the Commission of Fine Arts who favored modernism, however, continued to take Pope to task for his designs. Then the *Star* joined the fray against Pope and on 18 March 1937 Eames MacVeagh's diatribe reached the front page of the paper. Renderings of the Jefferson Memorial and the National Gallery occupied the center columns,

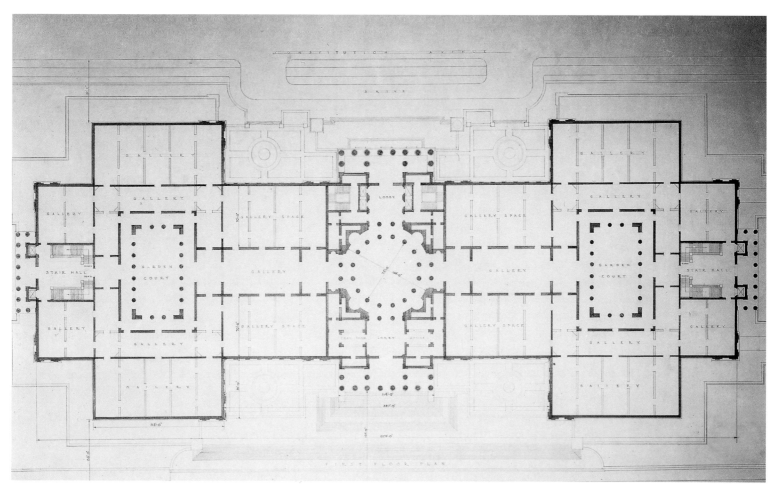

Fig. 7-30

with the caption: "Are These Two buildings Alike?"
Although the accompanying article focused on the
memorial, the design of the National Gallery of Art
had now become a public issue.

Seemingly undaunted, Pope presented his scheme
to the NCPPC, and predictably, he was asked to
increase the setback on the Mall side to conform
with the standard 100-foot line. Pope acceded to
this request, and in addition, he and Mellon reduced
the size of the building to a maximum width of just
over 300 feet and a length of 784 feet. Mellon, now
confident that there would be no further major
changes in design, authorized Pope to begin making
working drawings.

As Pope began his construction contract documents, Moore suggested that the three architect
members of the Commission of Fine Arts jointly
present their comments. In a letter, they questioned
the use of any major architectural decoration in the
principal interior spaces, such as the rotunda and
the two corridors leading to the rotunda, on the
grounds that this would compete with the artworks.
They expressed an intense dislike for skylights,
given their assumption that such a fenestration system would be hard to clean and maintain and would
hamper proper heating and cooling. They declared
the omission of a monumental stair on the Constitution Avenue side a major mistake, on the grounds
that many people would use this northern entrance
to avoid the monumental exterior stairs on the Mall
side. They insisted that the interior courts not be
covered. The side porticoes were described as superfluous. Pointing out that the dome would not line
up with the National Museum's dome, this triumvi-
rate, taking an unexpectedly classicist stance, pro-
nounced that the use of a dome to the east of the
National Museum would dictate that a dome be
used to the west as well. As a final point, they deni-
grated Pope's treatment of classical forms.

Having already begun working drawings, Pope
responded that he interpreted the commission's
demands for the dome and side entrances to be
removed as major changes in violation of the
approval already granted, and that, on the basis of
these earlier approvals, Mellon had already entered
into contract negotiations to erect the building.
Obviously, Pope and Mellon were unwilling to agree
to major changes, but at the same time, Pope was
making alterations to his design.

At the Commission of Fine Arts meeting in April
1937, Pope showed his initial schemes and some
progress sketches, which omitted the end porticoes,
made the dome wider and lower, added side light to
the basement galleries, and lowered the terrace approach walls. He responded to the objections about
the rotunda by explaining that no paintings would be
displayed there. He attempted to assure the Commission of Fine Arts that the issue of proper illumination

Fig. 7-31. National
Gallery of Art.
Entrance, mall
facade.

was well studied. His response to the issue of a monumental stair on the Constitution Avenue side of the building was emphatic and logical: since the main entrance to the Gallery was on the Mall side, he saw no need for another prominent entrance to the building. Using the example of the courtyard for the Frick Collection, Pope explained that the air-conditioned building would make the courtyard a pleasant place year-round, and that there would not be extensive plantings in the courtyards. Conceding the side porticoes, he showed the Commission of Fine Arts revised drawings without them.

On the issue of the dome, however, Pope's resistance increased. In response to the criticism, he retorted that it was a vital part of the building and its removal would destroy the design. He said he was prompted to design the building with a dome because McKim's plan for the Mall had proposed nine domed buildings in the vicinity of the Capitol. To his mind, a building lacking a dome would not have sufficient height to be appropriate for the site.

Nevertheless, Pope completed new studies for the Gallery in early June 1937, including perspective sketches and Mall elevations of the building both without a dome and with a reduced dome. When Pope sent these drawings to the Mellon trustees, he wrote that the scheme without the dome resulted in a monotonous interior plan, and furthermore, that it did not work with the adjacent buildings. Later in June, with ground-breaking having already begun, Andrew Mellon sent a very forceful letter to Charles Moore defending Pope's studies and conclusions. The Commission of Fine Arts, however, remained obdurate, one member stating that Pope had done a beautiful job of removing the dome. The members of the commission nevertheless seemed to realize that they were caught in a bind. They did not like the domical building, but Congress had in fact approved such a building, and the Commission of Fine Arts itself appeared to have done so the previous January. Recognizing their predicament, Moore reminded the members that their role was, after all, defined as only advisory. The Commission of Fine Arts met again in June and finally offered a resolution that would leave Mellon—who was by then in very poor health—free to do as he wished and proceed with his plans. By the time of the Commission of Fine Arts's final decision in July, Pope himself was suffering from a metastasizing abdominal cancer and had only a few months of painful life ahead of him.

Much of the interior design remained to be finalized and finishes had not yet been chosen when both Pope and Mellon died in late August 1937. With the original client and architect dead, a committee composed of, among others, the Gallery's first curator and various members of Pope's successor firm, Eggers and Higgins, finalized the design. Resolving many important interior design issues by using a large

Fig. 7-32. National Gallery of Art. Entrance, mall facade.

model whose interior could be modified, the group created a sumptuous interior, while on the exterior they removed the frieze inscriptions and sculpture from the aediculae.

As completed, the exterior is primarily Pope's. It is a marvel of severity. In overall form, he had deftly combined the organization and parti of Atwood's art museum with the monumental severity of Washington's early republican architecture as epitomized by George Hadfield's Old City Hall. Pope's careful application of water table, cornice mouldings, and channeled recesses represents a masterful handling of a vast blank wall. His pilaster-on-pilaster treatment of each corner niche added a bold chiaroscuro effect that marvelously articulated the corners of the building. As a result, it plays off as a strong edge against the National Archives and maintains the monumental image along the Mall. The stark severity of the building makes a quietly assertive statement and a masterful termination of this part of the Mall. Pope was correct about the dome: a long, low building could not have held its own in this position. It may emulate the Capitol, but it does not in any way challenge it.

Considering the concurrent uproar over Pope's Jefferson Memorial design, it is strange that, during his lifetime, the National Gallery's role in the bitter debate over modern versus classical design was a peripheral one. Although it was occasionally derided, the building was never at the center of the controversy over classicism until 1940. Even during the American Federation of the Arts convention in Washington in the spring of 1937, when champions of the International Style—Joseph Hudnut, then dean of Harvard's Graduate School of Design, and William Lescaze, the Swiss-born modernist designer of the Philadelphia Savings Fund Society building in Philadelphia—declared the irrelevance of classical Washington architecture, the National Gallery was hardly mentioned. The issue of the design of this public building still seemed a private matter between Pope, Mellon, and the Commission of Fine Arts.

It was not until 1940 that Hudnut began to criticize the National Gallery. In a scathing *House and Garden* article of July 1940, condemning the architecture of official Washington, he called it the "final disaster on the Mall." In the April 1941 issue of *Magazine of Art*, Hudnut published his now famous tract, "The Last of the Romans," which virtually guaranteed that Pope's work would soon sink into obscurity. In this short piece, Hudnut decried American classicism, charging that "an international style, based upon the study of the antique—generalized, documented, unweighted by reality, the work of esthetes rather than of builders—became the American Style." He attacked the elitist associations of classicism in general and declared its irrelevance to modern American society, and then went on to attack

the uninspired character of the interior arrangement of the National Gallery as having been designed with about as much architectural skill as that required to cut a cake. He echoed the standard modernist critique that cladding a steel structure in marble, giving the impression that it was a stone building, fooled no one and was a tired architectural lie. He bemoaned Pope's failure to express the vast array of modern machinery that was required to to maintain the appropriate environment. Identifying nine different styles in the Federal Triangle, nineteen facing the Mall, and three within the gallery itself, Hudnut pointed out that the need to conform to a prevailing style was, to his mind, a fallacy. He concluded the piece by saying that the modern style would soon be accepted in Washington, and that "surely the time cannot be far distant when we shall understand how inadequate is the death-mask of an ancient culture to express the heroic soul of America." With these words one of the most powerful men in architectural education had virtually destroyed Pope's reputation. From this moment forward he would be regarded as some sort of artistic dinosaur, an architectural reactionary who did not know when to quit.

Other equally critical assessments followed Hudnut's, and the National Gallery became the building that everyone loved to hate. The chief of the treasury's department's section of fine arts reportedly called the building a "pink marble whorehouse." In 1944 in the preface to his *Built in the U.S.A.*, Phillip Goodwin, co-architect of the Museum of Modern Art, referred to it as a "costly mummy." Students of these modernists wrote the next generation of American architectural histories and were merciless in their assessments of Pope. Today, however, we recognize the National Gallery as considerably more successful than the museums that modernism later inflicted on the Mall, such as Gordon Bunshaft's bunker-like Hirshhorn Museum, the cramped galleries of I. M. Pei's East Wing, or Gyo Obata's bland and gargantuan National Air and Space Museum.

The National Gallery was Pope's final act, demonstrating his remarkable ability to create, as an editorial in the *New York Times* of 29 August 1937 noted, "temples that sit serene in the moil and toil of modern commerce . . . [that] help express and interpret what has been called the sweeping orgy of architectural embellishment and aggrandizement of the era through which we have just lived and in which we still strive to come to grips with our national soul." But by then Pope was too late; his final statements of American classicism had become irrelevant to "modern" society.

Fig. 7-33. National Gallery of Art. Garden court.

Fig. 7-34. (Overleaf) National Gallery of Art. Rotunda.

CHAPTER 8

MONUMENTAL ARCHITECTURE 1913–37

T here was a great demand for monumental and memorial architecture between 1912 and 1937 as the United States became an important force in the world. There also was the coincidence of centennials and other major events that called for memorial architecture. Beginning with the centennial of the War of 1812 and the deaths or anniversaries of the deaths of important personages, numerous opportunities arose for the creation of monuments.

Pope's generation placed a premium on this form of architecture, both as the result of their predominantly Beaux-Arts-based training and the high cultural value that was placed on it. Up to World War I, with the successes of the Lincoln Memorial competition and the Temple of the Scottish Rite, Pope was frequently asked to enter competitions for major monumental works. Outside of official information filed with the AIA, virtually no record of his work or participation exists for many of these efforts. For some competitions, however, plentiful documentation exists.

Pope entered the competition for the Pulitzer Fountain (1913) at the Fifty-ninth Street entrance to Central Park in New York, one of the city's most famous public spaces, but his design was a disappointment and the jurors awarded the commission to Carrère and Hastings.

Pope's fortunes improved with the Thomas Macdonough memorials (1914–26) at Plattsburgh, New York, and Vergennes, Vermont. In 1913 and 1914, the United States Congress and the legislatures of Vermont and New York appropriated monies for the construction of two monuments to commemorate Commodore Macdonough's victory over the British in the naval battle of Plattsburgh, New York, on 11 September 1814. The War Department asked the Commission of Fine Arts to suggest advisors for the competition, and the names of William Mead, Bertram Goodhue, and Phillip Sawyer were provided. But after a year of inactivity, the War Department renewed its request and the Commission of Fine Arts suggested Henry Bacon, but no competition followed. Thomas Newton, the Army Corps

Fig. 8-1. Thomas Macdonough Memorial, Plattsburgh, New York, 1914–26.

of Engineers' district officer in Albany, in conjunction with his superiors, Colonel William M. Black and Major M. J. Macdonough in New York City, decided on a novel means of selecting the architect. Newton proposed to invite architects of a certain standing to compete for the commission by submitting photographs and documentation of their projects for commemorative monuments for review by the advisors. Pope was one of fifteen architects who were consulted. When they had seen his two Lincoln memorials, his Temple of the Scottish Rite, the William B. Leeds Tomb, and the Perry Memorial project, Pope was selected. In early 1917, Pope was ready to present his drawings to the Commission of Fine Arts, but the United States' entry into World War I delayed the review and approval of the project until 1919.

At Plattsburgh, Pope situated the memorial (fig. 8-1) opposite his city hall at the mouth of the Saranac River, overlooking the site of Macdonough's victory. The stepped peak of the 135-foot-high limestone obelisk and observation tower was topped by a bronze eagle signifying victory. Panels carved with swags terminated the obelisk. The 14-foot-square base, decorated with carved panels representing the implements of war, was topped by a horizontal cornice with corner acroteria. Above these panels were carved the names of the four principal ships of Macdonough's fleet—*Saratoga, Ticonderoga, Preble, and Eagle.* Above these, separated by a torus moulding, were the seals of the United States, the U.S. Navy, and the states of New York and Vermont. An extensive landscape plan included a large semicircular stone retaining wall with steps leading down to the river. As completed in 1926, the landscaping became a series of terraced earthen banks leading to the river.

In Vergennes, the granite-faced rectangular monument (fig. 8-2) was much more modest, but Pope placed it in the center of the Town Green. Four Doric columns, resting on a base in the shape of a large scotia moulding, support a stylized entablature. Bronze laurels above the columns ornament the corner of the frieze. The entablature is topped by

Fig. 8-2

Fig. 8-3

a large, low, triangular granite pediment that provides symbolic protection to a granite-faced panel
with a bronze bas-relief and lettered inscription commemorating Macdonough and his victory. Completed in 1925, this monument seems to have been
viewed through the filter of French neo-Grec style,
in which the influential forms are distilled to their
fundamental essences.

In designing funerary monuments, Pope persisted
in consulting antiquity for inspiration, heeding
Guadet's suggestion to create forms that inspired the
viewer to contemplate death. The William Charles
Stewart mausoleum (1915–16, fig. 8-3) in Woodlawn Cemetery, The Bronx, New York, was based
on the first century B.C. Temple of the Winds in
Athens. In Pope's rendition of the building, he ele-
vated it on a stone plinth decorated with squat
tripods, dispensed with the porches, and gave the
roof a steep pyramidal form. Although he maintained the character of the frieze and most of the
poses, his figures became feminine bearers of funerary flower wreaths. He omitted one figure altogether so that an identifying inscription could be
placed over the door. Although striking, it is perhaps
too direct a borrowing from antiquity and consequently is lacking in emotional force.

After providing the McLean family with a series

of elegant residences, Pope was asked in 1916 to
design their mausoleum (fig. 8-4). In the design for
this unbuilt project, he turned to ancient Egypt, proposing a short, squat monolithic obelisk raised on a
high, flared base. Hooded, winged figures reminiscent of Egyptian gods flanked a monumental opening composed of eared architraves and battered
antepagments that led to a deep vestibule containing
niches for funerary urns. At the terminus of the
vestibule was another door, presumably the entry to
the catacombs. If this had been been built, it would
have created a forceful impression far superior to
the Stewart mausoleum.

Pope's subsequent efforts, however, did not live up
to the promise of the McLean tomb. His F. W. Wool-
worth mausoleum (1919), also in Woodlawn Cemetery, projects a rather stilted and awkward feeling.
The Jules Bache mausoleum (c. 1919, fig. 8-5), again
in Woodlawn Cemetery, based on the Temple of Isis
on the Island of Phylae, is somewhat more successful, but is still too literal an interpretation to evoke
an emotional response.

The Egyptian did not seem to be the appropriate
model for the tomb of Pembroke Jones (1919),
Pope's father-in-law, in Wilmington, North Carolina. For this site, Pope instead created a dignified
composite of Roman and colonial revival forms.

Fig. 8-4

*Fig. 8-5. Jules
Bache mausoleum,
Woodlawn Cemetery,
The Bronx, New
York, c. 1919.*

Rising from a sloping water table, the Flemish-bond brick mass of the building is relieved by returns at each corner. The entrance, with its eared architrave and laurel-garlanded door, directly refers to Roman precedents, as do the clathri-muntined window and marble surrounds at the rear of the structure. Topped by a cross-gabled roof articulated as denticulated pediments, the structure maintains a severity of detail that is harmoniously coupled with the richness of color provided by the brick, creating a very peaceful image that is somehow appropriate in the lush landscape of Cape Fear.

The period from 1920 to 1925, when Pope was very active building country houses, corresponded to a lull in his work with monumental buildings. In 1925, this seemed to change when he competed for or was commissioned to work on five projects, ranging from the Huntington mausoleum in San Marino, California, to the Roosevelt memorials in New York and Washington, D.C. The first was the competition for the Marion, Ohio, mausoleum for President Warren G. Harding (1925), who had died in 1923. Mrs. Harding selected six architects to compete in a program that was rather vague, specifying only the cost of the proposed structure and the kind of drawings required. The triangular site was located near the juncture of two roads, with a ceremonial intersection planned at the entrance to the property and a pond at the other end.

Pope devised a scheme (fig. 8-6) placing the mausoleum at water's edge, with a long allée and reflecting pool connecting it to the major intersection. Pope conceived of the structure as a circular Doric double peristyle, in which large piers were alternated with columns on the interior row. He topped the peristyle with a ringed and imbricated dome, and the Doric entablature was topped by elaborate antefixes. The tomb itself was topped by a low, wide tripod based on that of the Roman general Cornelius Scipio Barbatus. But despite the obvious merits of such a design, Pope had made a fatal error in designing a domed structure as a memorial for the man whose administration was rocked by the Teapot Dome scandal.

After railroad magnate Henry H. Huntington's wife, Arabella, died in 1924, he decided to glorify their San Marino, California, estate with a mausoleum. With the idea of building a classical temple, he solicited Duveen's advice in August of 1925. In a telegram to Huntington dated 1 August 1925, Duveen recommended Pope as the "greatest architect of modern times and the only man for you." Shortly thereafter Pope was hired.

From the very beginning, Pope had in mind the creation of a composite mausoleum and garden temple (fig. 8-7). The first scheme comprised a circular Tuscan peristyle supporting a dome, but this was soon abandoned for a much larger circular building,

*Fig. 8-6. Proposal for
Warren G. Harding
Memorial (unbuilt),
Marion, Ohio, 1925.*

in which Pope supplants the Tuscan with his favorite Roman Ionic from the Theater of Marcellus.

Pope received Huntington's approval to hire a sculptor to assist in the decoration and help with the model, and again with the counsel of Duveen, John Gregory, a fellow of the American Academy in Rome, was chosen. But delays in Gregory's work slowed construction, and Huntington died almost two years before the mausoleum was completed in 1929.

The mausoleum closely follows the model, evincing only some minor changes in the decoration. Pope's design was not only related to his own earlier work in Roman and eighteenth-century French idioms, but also to Nicholas Hawksmoor's mausoleum (1742) for Castle Howard at York, and James Wyatt's at Brocklesby Park (1794). He had developed a parti that was almost perfect for any sort of centralized monument, and would apply it on several more commissions, including the Jefferson Memorial.

In late 1928, the trustees of the Grant Memorial Association attempted to raise funds to complete complete Grant's Tomb (originally designed by John Duncan, and mostly completed by 1913) in New York. After Pope's selection, he prepared a simple plan that called for a sculpted marble pediment over the Doric entry portico, a large terrace flanked by a low granite wall and adorned with an equestrian statue of Grant raised on a large base (fig. 8-8). However, sufficient funds could not be raised before the advent of the Depression, and the project never came to fruition.

In the Resthaven Mausoleum (1925–27) in Resthaven Cemetery, Elmont, Long Island, Pope was faced with developing a scheme for dealing with mortal remains on massive scale, and arrived at a very simple parti: a centrally planned funerary chapel flanked by vast wings to accommodate catacombs (fig. 8-9). The first scheme was reduced by shortening the wings and recasting the central element, with the dome replaced by a low, stepped pyramidal form. Just as the Huntington mausoleum was the springboard for much of Pope's later work, in this design, a parti emerges that Pope frequently would use in future work, particularly in his museums, and especially in the Tate Gallery, the Frick Collection, and the National Gallery of Art, where the corner aediculae and central motif become stock items. When surviving employees of the firm were questioned about this similarity of forms, they responded that, when one is faced with designing a building with a central entry and wings, there are limited number of classical solutions, regardless of the building type.

As a member of the Commission of Fine Arts, Pope played an active role in the design of the American

Fig. 8-8

Fig. 8-8. Proposal
for completion
of Grant's Tomb
(unbuilt), New York,
1928.

Fig. 8-9. Resthaven
Mausoleum, Elmont,
New York, 1925–27.
Rendering for initial
scheme.

Fig. 8-9

war cemeteries in France. Although the War Department financed repatriation of the remains of American war dead, the potential cost of returning approximately 84,000 bodies, and the unsavory experience of the Spanish-American War dead having been left unclaimed on the wharfs of San Francisco, led the War Department to establish permanent American cemeteries in Europe. To this end, Charles Platt was asked to design headstones and Pope was asked to collaborate in developing a central motif that could be used in each of the cemeteries. Since it was envisioned that all of the American dead, in the manner of Arlington National Cemetery, would be concentrated in six or seven separate sites in a variety of terrains, Pope and Platt devised a simple circular walk that surrounded a flagpole with a prominent base. Pope's studies were approved and eventually adopted.

His most famous war memorial was in France, at Montfauçon (fig. 8-10). In 1923, Congress created the American Battle Monuments Commission (ABMC) to take over two separate World War I memorial projects of the War Department, one for military cemeteries, the other for commemorating the French and Belgian battlefields with stone and bronze maps.

As an expression of national pride, and perhaps in reaction to the grandiose British memorials, the ABMC decided to build monuments where American troops had played an important military role. Eleven sites were selected, including Aisne-Marne, Saint-Mihiel, and Montfauçon, which were slated to receive major monuments. Paul Cret was chosen as advisory architect, and, by the end of November 1925, Pope had been assigned the monument at Montfauçon. Since this was the site of the largest American operation, the ABMC wanted it to be the largest of the three monuments and the site was given the largest budget.

Pope was ready to submit drawings in early October 1926. He sent sketches of three schemes to the ABMC in Washington. The first scheme was a simple wall about 22 feet high, with a suitable inscription and a figure positioned at each end resting against a pylon. The second scheme was a Doric column about 24 feet in diameter surmounted by a large figure. The third scheme, the most unconventional of all, was shaped like a truncated, stepped obelisk. With these three schemes, Pope had delivered a wide range of alternatives, from the simplest possible, to an expected solution (the Doric column shaft), to one of incredible complexity that seemed to have been inspired by both Mayan and Egyptian architecture. At a meeting that was held on 21 December 1926, the ABMC, along with Cret, voted for Pope's column by a margin of eight to one.

Sketches were completed and presented to the ABMC in early January 1928, and the preliminary

work continued without complication until late 1930. Then, citing excessive costs, the ABMC decided to omit the landscaping and approach to the structure. They pressured Pope to approve additional inscriptions around the base of the column and on the plaza. There were continual mistakes made in the stone cutting. And, as a final insult, the figure to be placed atop the column was assembled facing the wrong way and had to be reset. The commission was becoming an embarrassment to Pope. The ABMC failed to recognize the design as a set of carefully linked components, in which any change necessitated adjustments in the rest of the design. They tended to treat the work as a series of autonomous elements and tinkered with each as they pleased. This frustrated Pope and partially thwarted the effect of his original grand vision. The result, although forceful and monumental, falls far short of Pope's original idea, which was sullied by too many attempts to add to the building.

While work on Montfauçon was in its earliest stages, the New York State Theodore Roosevelt Memorial (1925–33, fig. 8-11) came to fruition. As completed, it is Pope's only major monumental work in New York City. In May 1919, following Roosevelt's death, the president of the American Museum of Natural History, Henry Fairfield Osborne, proposed that the memorial to Roosevelt form part of the museum, since Roosevelt led one of the museum's expeditions to South America, and his father was one of the founders of the institution.

In 1922, Osborne published plans for a memorial that was to serve as the Central Park West entrance to the museum. It was also envisioned as a terminus for a proposed "museum walk" that would cut a formal allée across Central Park to connect with the Metropolitan Museum on Fifth Avenue. Although the state capital at Albany was initially considered as a site, Osborne's lobbying won the memorial for New York. Governor Alfred E. Smith appointed a board of trustees, who held an invitational competition for the design of the monument. Pope, along with seven other firms, was selected to compete. The program dictated that "the design should symbolize the scientific, educational, outdoor, and exploration aspects of Theodore Roosevelt's life rather than the political and literary." Furthermore, the jurors desired a scheme that would harmonize with the existing museum.

Pope's solution to this program was to ignore it. Seizing on the image of Roosevelt as benevolent conqueror and the creator of an imperial image of America, Pope elected to commemorate him in an appropriately Roman manner. Borrowing forms of the imperial Roman arch and bath, he created a powerfully monumental entrance for the museum in the form of a triumphal arch, which was also the perfect terminus for the long allée proposed as the western terminus of Osborne's museum walk. Pope

*Fig. 8-10. Montfauçon
Memorial, Montfauçon,
France, 1925–35.*

Fig. 8-11. New York State Theodore Roosevelt Memorial, New York, 1925–33.

suggested that a concourse 160 feet wide and 500 feet long be run along Central Park West Drive in front of the museum. The entrance was to come forward and break from the established building line, being reached by a large granite terrace, in the center of which would be an equestrian statue of Roosevelt flanked by figures of a Native American and a "primitive African." Each of the six projecting columns decorating the exterior arch was to be topped by heroic figures representing the different phases of Roosevelt's life. The only gesture to the existing building was Pope's selection of pink granite for the exterior, which matched the stone used for the flanking wings. Pope successfully satisfied the circulatory functions of the entrance by creating a series of galleries and stairs separate from the main hall, which accommodated the six floors of exhibition halls and the subway entrance connected to the memorial at four different points. The interior memorial hall was a vast barrel-vaulted room decorated with huge Tuscan columns topped by figures of eagles alternating with murals depicting important moments in Roosevelt's life, while animals, stuffed and mounted on pedestals, completed the image.

After seemingly violating the program in virtually every respect, in early June 1925 Pope was announced as the winner. In contrast to his fellow competitors, who failed to recognize the importance of glorifying Roosevelt and paid too much homage to the existing structure, Pope provided an image of a prominent and separate memorial to Roosevelt. By acknowledging the museum promenade, he played to the interests of the influential president of the museum.

More importantly, he also created an imperial image that appealed to the jurors.

Once Pope won the competition, the proposal was further refined, particularly on the interior, where a number of changes were made. The scheme was approved by the trustees in December 1925. However, by spring, Pope was already asking to change the stone to be used for the exterior cladding. Citing the high cost of Picton Island red granite, which would have harmonized more with the flanking wings, Pope asked for and was granted a change to Milford red granite. This may have seemed like a minor adjustment at the time, but it was actually quite important, because Milford granite fades to white and thus would eventually set off Pope's design from the rest of the building.

It would be almost five more years before the building was completed and dedicated by President Franklin D. Roosevelt and Governor Herbert Lehman. One reaches the building via a terraced approach protected by a parapet wall with bas-reliefs of some of Roosevelt's favorite game animals. The columns of the arch are topped by figures of Audubon, Boone, and Lewis and Clark. Each aedicule, as well as the flooring pattern, is borrowed from the Pantheon, and even the eagle and wreath bas-reliefs are based on those in Trajan's Forum, while other designs were borrowed from the works of d'Espouy.

The building is one of Pope's most distinguished, and, as one of the few examples of his monumental work that reached full fruition without interference from institutional or governmental committees, it is a rare example of a fully realized monument design by Pope.

In Washington, D.C., the Roosevelt Memorial Association, founded in 1920, lobbied Congress to allow them to hold a competition for a memorial, with the south axis of the White House, on the Tidal Basin, as their site. In 1925, the Association was granted permission to use the site, but final approval was reserved until a design was ratified by Congress. Pope competed against seven other architects and won in October 1925.

Here Pope was faced with a site that had much in common with those of the Lincoln Memorial, the Huntington mausoleum, and the Harding memorial. Each had to accommodate more than one axis, with the primary axis emphasized but not terminated, which meant there could be no central focal point. For his solution (fig. 8-12), Pope designed a circular fountain 280 feet in diameter from which a jet was to rise 200 feet. At the four compass points rose prows of stylized classical galleys ferrying the allegorical figures of Art, Government, Science, and Industry. The fountain, in turn, was surrounded by a basin 600 feet in diameter flanked by two 60-foot-high double colonnades describing 90° arcs of a circle 800 feet in diameter.

Because the final approval of Pope's design lay with Congress, Pope was concerned that the monument would never be built, particularly since Congress was controlled by what he described as Wilsonian Democrats. Despite Pope's worries, the project was praised by the architectural press, but the issue of the appropriation for its completion was stalled in the House Library Committee. Because Jefferson was not honored on the Mall, the Committee was reluctant to give a major site to another Republican, let alone one who ran against Wilson. Instead, the Committee authorized the drafting of a resolution for a Jefferson Memorial. The case for the Roosevelt Memorial was not aided by the fact that Mrs. Roosevelt herself was opposed to it. Congress allowed the proposal to die in committee.

With the rise of the modern movement in America, more and more critics expressed dislike for Pope's work. Construction of the New York State Theodore Roosevelt Memorial occurred exactly at the same time that much of New York's design community was beginning to adopt the International Style. As the building slowly grew, so did the resistance to its classical design, and the death of this project seemed to be a harbinger of Pope's future difficulties with major commissions in large cities.

In the late 1920s and early 1930s, Pope was for the most part spared the savage criticism of modernists

Fig. 8-12. Proposal for Theodore Roosevelt Memorial (unbuilt), Washington, D.C., 1925.

215

as he focused on smaller commissions, such as the competition for Revolutionary War hero George Rogers Clark's memorials in Indiana (1930) and Pennsylvania (1931, fig. 8-13); and the memorial in Washington, D.C., to the distinguished statesman, jurist, and diplomat Oscar A. Strauss (fig. 8-14), which as completed in 1947 only provides faint echoes of Pope's initial design.

Although primarily involved with monumental buildings or structures, Pope was distressed by the various encroachments of temporary government buildings on the Mall, and he personally lobbied President Roosevelt to promote the completion of the Mall by ordering their removal. Roosevelt complied, and by early 1936, many of the buildings were gone. As a result, Pope had a lasting and almost unacknowledged effect on one of America's greatest public spaces.

The Jefferson Memorial (1935–37, completed 1943) (figs. 8-15–8-21), the last of Pope's monumental works, is also the most problematic. It was conceived, along with other major projects such as the Federal Reserve Board building and the National Gallery of Art, during a time when classicism was becoming more and more discredited. In accepting to work with the Jefferson Memorial Commission, Pope could be certain that he would be drawn into conflict with modernists.

This issue of a memorial to Jefferson had been under consideration by the Commission of Fine Arts since 1914, when it had suggested that a monument be placed at Union Station or close to the Department of State building. The subject lay fallow until January 1934, when President Roosevelt wrote to Charles Moore asking the Commission of Fine Arts to study the possibility of placing a Jefferson memorial on the triangular site east of the National Archives building. Moore replied on behalf of the Commission of Fine Arts that the site should be reserved for the proposed Apex building, and ended the letter with the Commission of Fine Arts's polite suggestion that perhaps the president should take the issue up with Congress. Roosevelt replied that he liked the idea of locating it on the cross-axis of the Mall, opposite the National Archives, and shortly afterwards, the Jefferson Memorial Commission was formed. Its enabling legislation called for the appointment of twelve commissioners, senators, members of the House, the undersecretary of the Treasury Department, and three other appointees, including architect Fiske Kimball, an expert on Jefferson's architecture and director of the Philadelphia Museum of Art.

Kimball showed himself to be willing to push for an extremely large memorial in a location of great prominence, and suggested the Tidal Basin at the southern end of the White House cross-axis of the Mall, which was the last important site left. He further strongly recommended that the building be a domed Roman hall in deference to Jefferson's admiration of the Pantheon.

At the Memorial Commission's first meeting on 12 April 1935, the commissioners deferred to Kimball. No other members brought up the issue of style, and henceforth, the commission refused to entertain suggestions of any other styles. Kimball also pressed for the Tidal Basin as the site and brought up Pope's name in connection with his other memorial designs for Washington. The members of the Memorial Commission then agreed to

*Fig. 8-13.
Proposal for
George Rogers Clark
Memorial (unbuilt),
Harrodsburg,
Pennsylvania, 1931*

Fig. 8-14. *Oscar Strauss Memorial, Washington, D.C., 1931–47. Rendering for initial scheme.*

consult with the Commission of Fine Arts and the National Capital Park and Planning Commission, and to consider the president's views as well as consult with him. Finally, the Memorial Commission voted to tentatively approve the Tidal Basin as the site. It was then announced that Pope had been invited to address their next meeting.

When Pope appeared, he led a lengthy discussion of Jefferson's role in the development of American architecture, followed by an exhaustive evaluation of each of the four sites being considered. He believed that since Jefferson was the progenitor of American classicism, the architect of his memorial must be sympathetic to the pure classical architecture he revered.

In discussing each site, Pope betrayed a particular interest in the Tidal Basin and National Archives cross-axis site. The members of the Memorial Commission were suitably impressed by him, and he was retained to make preliminary studies. He developed four ideal, site-specific designs, each of which solved its location's unique problems. The site on the Tidal Basin was absolutely in accordance the McMillan plan. In Pope's proposal, the center line of the portico of the memorial was aligned directly on axis with the White House, almost a half mile away, while the diagonal axis to the Capitol, via Maryland Avenue, intersected with the center of the circular building. The memorial would be stupendous, 220 feet in diameter and 144 feet high. The costs were equally high, over nine million dollars.

Pope's drawings were sent to Washington, where they were set up in the diplomatic reception room of the White House (the Red Room) where President Roosevelt, Pope, and the full membership of the Memorial Commission reviewed them. Roosevelt expressed a preference for the Tidal Basin site, but, on hearing of the costs, asked that they be scaled back to the three million dollars allocated in the original legislation. Pope was reluctant to develop further studies, and contention arose between himself, President Roosevelt, and the Memorial Commission. Most of the members seemed to think that, despite Pope's higher projected costs, three million dollars was adequate to produce an appropriate memorial, and Kimball agreed to ask Pope to try to develop a design that would cost no more than that. Pope acquiesced, and, concentrating on the Tidal Basin design, reduced its size by twenty percent.

At this point it was Kimball, however, and not Pope, who made the initial suggestions for the shape of the building. Kimball proposed that Pope develop a building on a Greek cross plan that would emulate Palladio's Villa Rotunda, one of Jefferson's favorite buildings. Pope, however, wanted to continue to refine his circular Pantheon-based scheme. Kimball had no objection, and by early September 1936 the two design schemes were virtually finished.

The first scheme, based on the Pantheon and George Hadfield's Old City Hall, was simply a reduced version of the original circular scheme. The

Figs. 8-15–8-18.
Proposed schemes for
Jefferson Memorial,
Washington, D.C.,
1935–37 (completed
1943).

interior was to be 90 feet in diameter and 100 feet high. The outside colonnade would be 165 feet in diameter. Including the base it rested on, the building was to rise to a height of 136 feet—the same height as the Lincoln Memorial. In the second scheme, the scale and height of the interior were identical, but on the exterior, in the manner of the Villa Rotunda, Pope replaced the circular colonnade with four identical Ionic porticoes.

Pope's estimates for the buildings came in under the three-million-dollar ceiling, but the necessary landscape improvements amounted to another one and one half million dollars. This caused a certain amount of concern among the members of the Memorial Commission until it was learned that the costs could be allotted so that, once the memorial was begun, further appropriations could be obtained for landscaping and terracing, which is how the Lincoln Memorial was in fact paid for.

The Memorial Commission unanimously approved both the site and the circular design, and then proposed that Pope be named as architect, a motion that also carried unanimously. The National Park Service was then designated as the agency that would oversee the contract. With this last motion, the Thomas Jefferson Memorial Commission concluded its business. By the following day, the design was published in the newspaper, and it was then that the furor began.

Fig. 8-19.
Jefferson Memorial.

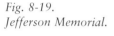

Local newspapers began to criticize the location and design of the building, and public opinion slowly rose up against Pope's work. Public sentiment also focused on the possible loss of Japanese cherry trees caused by the planned reshaping of the Tidal Basin. A gift from the city of Tokyo, the trees in blossom had become a lucrative tourist attraction, and any threat to the economy of Washington was not welcomed. With the country still in the midst of a serious depression, the most vituperative criticism came from a group composed largely of advocates for the housing division of the Public Works Administration and proponents of the modern movement, including Catherine Bauer, Henry Churchill, Carl Feiss, Talbot Hamlin, Joseph Hudnut, William Lescaze, and Lewis Mumford.

The League for Progress in Architecture codified a series of objections that would be reiterated by individual members in influential periodicals and at important meetings. For them, Pope's design was entirely inappropriate and completely without vitality or imagination. The memorial would serve no purpose whatsoever, particularly in light of the fact that two-thirds of the nation was inadequately fed, clothed, and housed. Also, the site would create massive traffic problems, and finally, there had been no competition. The group also took its complaints directly to the president.

It was against this hostile background that the various governing bodies began the debate over the

memorial. The Commission of Fine Arts, however, was still committed to Jefferson's image of a Washington graced by classical-style buildings. And while the Architectural League of New York and the National Sculpture Society approved of Pope's work, the attacks continued. The faculty of the School of Architecture at Columbia, Pope's alma mater, condemned his design to a *Star* reporter on 31 March 1937 as a "lamentable misfit in time and place." Frank Lloyd Wright, on 30 March 1937, in a letter to President Roosevelt, described the work as an "arrogant insult to the memory of Thomas Jefferson." The memorial began to attract national attention with *Time*, *Christian Science Monitor*, and *Literary Digest* carrying news articles on it, and local papers also kept up the heat.

The criticism began to take a toll on Pope, who was already dying from abdominal cancer. He contributed to the difficulties by staying out of the public fray. However, he continued to meet quietly at private clubs with members of the Commission of Fine Arts and other influential friends. The general reaction to Pope's detractors among his friends was quite well summed up by Egerton Swartwout, who observed in a letter dated 19 April 1937 to Charles Moore that those who were opposed to the design for the Jefferson Memorial were "architects and engineers that are on relief. Nobody of consequence at all, but they make a great deal of noise like all minorities."

Maneuvering in Congress continued through the rest of April and May 1937. In late April, a torrent of letters opposing Pope's appointment as architect for the memorial was presented at a House hearing, letters from a vast number of luminaries, including the director of the Museum of Modern Art, Alfred H. Barr Jr., architects Eli Jacques Kahn, William Lescaze, and Henry Churchill, historian Talbot Hamlin, and painter Max Weber. Opposition continued to grow in the House, and the hearings continued with a vast procession of organizations protesting the project's costs and universal objection to the loss of the cherry trees. The project seemed completely doomed when the House Appropriations Committee withheld the money requested to begin construction. Pope was now about to be thwarted by cherry trees.

Few offered any defense of him, and an incessant litany of criticism continued. With political action going against the memorial, more and more well-known architects and arts organizations began to weigh in against the project and Pope's architecture in general. The most telling blows were delivered during the Washington convention of the American Federation of the Arts in May of 1937. Noted modernist architects William Lescaze and Joseph Hudnut both spoke out against the memorial with such conviction that their speeches were later published in the Federation's *Magazine of Art*. They both rejected Pope's work as inappropriate to its own time, and elaborated by claiming that it did not, by any token, grow out of contemporary life; that it did not fulfill the requirements of contemporary life; that it did not make good use of contemporary methods of construction; and that classical architecture had turned Washington from the executive seat of democracy into the Rome of an empire.

Pope responded with silence. Not only was he ill, but he was a designer, not a theorist. He had embraced classicism wholeheartedly and unquestioningly and lacked both the inclination and the theoretical grounding to respond to the modernist polemic. However, he hung on for the project, but by this time it had temporarily become a lost cause. In August 1937, Congress deleted the appropriation for the memorial and Pope's firm was ordered to cease work on 23 August. Four days later, Pope was dead.

The work did go on, but it was Pope's in name only. Successors Eggers and Higgins agreed to restudy the design, and since Pope's widow, Sadie, was still heir to Pope's rights to these works, she was consulted. She insisted that the memorial take the form of the Pantheon-based scheme, and to advance her cause she mounted a successful letter-writing campaign to President Roosevelt, a distant relative by marriage. A reduced version of Pope's Pantheon-based scheme was eventually adopted and built at the edge of the Tidal Basin. And, with the United States by then at war with Japan, any loss of the cherry trees was ignored.

The Jefferson Memorial has now become one of the major icons of the city of Washington. However, in terms of Pope's work, it is hardly his. Most strikingly, its proportions demonstrate a certain lack of sensitivity. However, it does bear the characteristics of the original parti, even though it is but a weak shadow of the normally forceful and austere monumentality that was Pope's trademark.

Pope's monumental work from after 1912 displays certain consistencies. First, there was a compelling treatment of basic form, or massing, that gave all of his monuments—large and small—great power. Given that he constantly limited his architectural vocabulary to the idiom of classical architecture, his work often showed a surprising degree of creativity. Pope's later works, however, demonstrate a very limited imagination. His constant reworking of certain forms could be interpreted either as a lack of creativity, or, more positively, as an urge to perfect an ideal form. At his best, Pope produced brilliant schemes, but his continuous reliance on precedent may indicate that he was never able to control the feelings of insecurity that Austin Lord had first observed while he was still a student at the American School of Architecture in Rome.

Upon Pope's death, the tide had turned against the kind of architecture he practiced and his work

Fig. 8-20.
Jefferson Memorial.

had lost a degree of relevancy. However, in terms of longevity, he was truly the last of the great classical designers. The major designers who outlived him never created monuments equal to Pope's. His career neatly spanned the entire period during which classicism was the most important influence, from the Chicago fair of 1893 to his last two buildings, the National Gallery of Art and the Jefferson Memorial.

It was William Adams Delano, in his "Memoirs of Centurian Architects" (*Journal of the AIA*, August 1948), who answered the question of how Pope ranked with his contemporaries: Delano properly noted that, with the exception of those who dared to reinterpet classicism, Pope was the best of his generation. Pope could interpret classical forms, and developed in his work a more American classical idiom by borrowing from the chaste forms of early nineteenth-century American architecture.

There is no doubt that Pope's individual approach to classicism, expressed in its characteristically monumental and severe manner, captured the interest and appeal of his clients and the architectural press. The Temple of the Scottish Rite is still regarded as one of America's greatest architectural achievements. His masterful handling of materials was unrivaled among his peers. His planning skills were more than adequate to meet the demands of most of the tasks set before him. His sense of proportion and his ability to create dignified, refined, and functional structures is unquestioned. For him, precedent was law, and there is no doubt that in this belief he obeyed the planning principles of his French academic training. Still, with his lengthy, successful career and distinctive style, Pope emerged as the quintessential American classical architect of the first part of this century.

Fig. 8-21.
Jefferson Memorial.

CHRONOLOGY
OF BUILDINGS

Since Pope's office records were mostly destroyed following his death, it is not possible to compile an absolutely complete list of projects undertaken by him or his firm. The following list represents all of the buildings discussed in this book and others of minor importance.

1895	Proposal for a chapel for Alfred Loomis (unbuilt), Ringwood, New Jersey.
c. 1900	George St. George house, Tuxedo Park, New York (with office of Bruce Price).
1900	Detroit Bicentennial Memorial Column, Detroit, Michigan (with McKim, Mead & White).
1900	*Ladies' Home Journal* Georgian House for $7,000 (with office of Bruce Price).
1900–01	Washington County Library, Hagerstown, Maryland (with office of Bruce Price).
1901	Kingscote (Kingdon Gould house), Lakewood, New Jersey (with office of Bruce Price).
1901	Proposal for New York Custom House (unbuilt), New York (with office of Bruce Price).
1901	Proposal for New York Stock Exchange (unbuilt), New York (with office of Bruce Price).
1901	Willard Humphreys house, Princeton, New Jersey.
1901	Proposal for City Hall (unbuilt), Wilkes-Barre, Pennsylvania (with office of Bruce Price).
1901–03	Dr. and Mrs. Henry Barton Jacobs house, Newport, Rhode Island.
1902	Perrin house, Washington, D.C. (with office of Bruce Price).
1903	McLean house, Washington, D.C.
1903	W. L. Stow house, Roslyn, New York.
1904–08	Freedman's Hospital, Washington, D.C. (with office of Bruce Price).
1905	Design for a Commemorative Monument on the Great Lakes.
1905	Jacobs house, Baltimore, Maryland.
1905–06	Gate house, William K. Vanderbilt Jr. estate, Long Neck, New York.
1906	Belmont Farm, Long Island, New York.
1906	Middleton Burrill house, Jericho, New York.
1907	Addition to Belcort Castle, Newport, Rhode Island.
1907	Arlough (Robert Low Bacon house), Westbury, New York.
1907	Long Island country house projects.
1907	John Roll McLean house, Washington, D.C.
1907	George Howard house, Washington, D.C. (begun with office of Bruce Price).
1907	W. Storrs Wells house, New York.
1907	Proposal for William B. Leeds house (unbuilt), New York.
1907–09	Mrs. R. R. Hitt house, Washington, D.C.
1907–09	William B. Leeds mausoleum, Woodlawn Cemetery, The Bronx, New York.
1908	Chateauiver (Charles Gould house), Greenlawn, New York.
1908	Proposal for Poetram house (unbuilt), New York.
Begun 1908	Lincoln Birthplace Museum, Hodgenville, Kentucky.
1909	Chapel, Westbury, New York.
1909	Proposal for Rector's Hotel (unbuilt), New York.
1910	Lord Memorial Fountain, Somerville, New Jersey.
1910	Peter Fenelon Collier mausoleum, Wickatunk, New Jersey.
Begun 1910	De Koven house, New York.
1910–12	Henry White house, Washington, D.C.
1910–16	Temple of the Scottish Rite, Washington, D.C.
1911	Robert J. Collier Jr. house, Wickatunk, New Jersey.
1911	Virginia Graham Fair Vanderbilt house, Old Westbury, New York.
1911–12	Proposal for Lincoln Memorial (unbuilt), Washington, D.C.

1912	Irvin commission, location unknown.
1912	Levi P. Morton house, Washington, D.C.
1912	Robert S. McCormick house, Washington, D.C.
1912	Scheftel project, location unknown.
1912–14	George Hewitt Myers house, Washington, D.C.
1912–14	Bonniecrest (Stuart Duncan house), Newport, Rhode Island.
1913	Branch house, Richmond, Virginia.
1913	Proposal for post office (unbuilt), Portland, Oregon.
1913	Proposal for Pulitzer Memorial Fountain (unbuilt), New York.
1913–19	Union Station, Richmond, Virginia.
c. 1914	Temple of Love, Jones estate, Wilmington, North Carolina.
1914	Charlcote (James Swan Frick house), Baltimore, Maryland.
1914	Proposal for George Washington Memorial Hall (unbuilt), Washington, D.C.
1914–25	Thomas Macdonough Memorial, Vergennes, Vermont.
1914–26	Thomas Macdonough Memorial, Plattsburgh, New York.
c. 1915	Addition to Chateau Sur Mer, Newport, Rhode Island.
c. 1915	Addition to Garvan house, Roslyn, New York.
c. 1915	Addition to T. Suffern Tailer house, Newport, Rhode Island.
1915	A. S. Williams house, Wilmington, North Carolina.
1915	Robert Low Bacon Jr. house, Westbury, New York.
1915	Arthur Scott Burden house, Jericho, New York.
1915	Proposal for Fourth Regiment Armory (unbuilt), Baltimore, Maryland.
1915	Ogden Mills house, Woodbury, New York.
1915	Proposal for Newark Memorial Building (unbuilt), Newark, New Jersey.
1915	Proposal for house for Prince Christopher of Greece (unbuilt), New York.
1915–16	William Charles Stewart mausoleum, Woodlawn Cemetery, The Bronx, New York.
1915–17	H. L. Dulin house, Knoxville, Tennessee.
1915–17	Kamp Kill Kare (renovation for Francis Patrick Garvan), near Raquette Lake, New York.
c. 1915–19	Proposal for a bank building (probably Redmond Bank; unbuilt), New York.
c. 1916	Proposal for John R. McLean Memorial (unbuilt), Cincinnati, Ohio.
1916	Proposal for Cleveland Public Library (unbuilt), Cleveland, Ohio.
1916	Proposal for Jacksonville Terminal (unbuilt), Jacksonville, Florida.
1916	Proposal for Mclean mausoleum (unbuilt).
1916–17	Allan S. Lehman house, Tarrytown, New York.
1916–18	Chapel at Kamp Kill Kare, near Raquette Lake, New York.
1916–20	City Hall, Plattsburgh, New York.
1917	Proposal for Francis Patrick Garvan house (unbuilt), New York.
1917	Merleigh Farm (William F. Hencken house), Greenwich, Connecticut.
1917	J. Randolph Robinson house, Westbury, New York.
1917	Scott house, Royal Orchard, Virginia.
1917	Andrew Varick Stout house, Red Bank, New Jersey.
1917	Sketch for remodeling of State, War and Navy Building, Washington, D.C.
1917–18	George Hewitt Myers house, Watch Hill, Rhode Island.
1917–19	Plan for Yale University, New Haven, Connecticut.
1918	Proposed city market, New York.
c. 1919	Jules Bache mausoleum, Woodlawn Cemetery, The Bronx, New York.
1919	Bull house, Ardmore, Pennsylvania.
1919	F. W. Woolworth mausoleum, Woodlawn Cemetery, The Bronx, New York.
1919	Proposal for Nebraska state capitol (unbuilt), Omaha, Nebraska.
1919	Pembroke Jones mausoleum, Wilmington, North Carolina.
1919–21	Thomas Frothingham/John Sloan House, Far Hills, New Jersey.
1919–22	Irwin Boyle Laughlin house, Washington, D.C.
c. 1920	Proposal for Massachusetts Bonding Insurance Company (unbuilt), New York.
c. 1920	Proposal for skyscraper (unbuilt), New York.
c. 1920	Temple of the Scottish Rite Consistory, Washington, D.C.
1920	Chapel at Old Westbury, New York.
c. 1920–22	Tenacre (Joseph Knapp house), Southampton, New York.
1920–30	Caumsett (Marshall Field II estate), Huntington, New York.
1921	Proposed plan for Dartmouth College (unbuilt), Hanover, New Hampshire.
1921–36	Second Division Memorial, Washington, D.C.
1922–27	Glen Farm (Moses Taylor house), near Newport, Rhode Island.
1922–29	Proposed plan for Syracuse University (unbuilt), Syracuse, New York (with Dwight James Baum).
1923–24	John F. Wilkins house, Rockville, Maryland.
c. 1924	J. H. Carstairs house, Ardmore, Pennsylvania.
1924	Addition to Hugh J. Chisholm house, Port Chester, New York.
1924	Larchmont Avenue Presbyterian Church, Larchmont, New York.
1924	John Russell Pope house, New York.
1924	Proposed plan for The Johns Hopkins University (unbuilt), Baltimore, Maryland.
1924	Proposal for Masonic Temple (unbuilt), Toledo, Ohio.
1924–28	Skylands Farm (Clarence Lewis house), near Sterlington, New York, and Ringwood, New Jersey.
1924–32	Constitution Hall, Washington, D.C.
1924/28	Harriman/Heckscher building, New York.
c. 1925	W. T. Richard house, York Harbor, Maine.
c. 1925	Church, Lubbock, Texas.
1925	Seward Pulitzer house, Wheatley Hills, New York.
1925	Wayne Johnson house, Southampton, New York.
1925	Proposal for Warren G. Harding Memorial (unbuilt), Marion, Ohio.
1925	Proposal for Theodore Roosevelt Memorial (unbuilt), Washington, D.C.
1925	Tudor country house, Tuxedo Park, New York.
1925–26	University Club, Milwaukee, Wisconsin.
1925–27	Resthaven Mausoleum, Elmont, New York.
1925–28	University Baptist Church, Baltimore, Maryland.
1925–29	Huntington mausoleum, San Marino, California.
1925–33	Baltimore Museum of Art, Baltimore, Maryland.
1925–33	New York State Theodore Roosevelt Memorial, New York.
1925–35	Montfauçon Memorial, Montfauçon, France.
1926	Consuelo Vanderbilt Smith apartment, New York.
1926	Port of the Missing Men (Col. H. H. Rogers house), Southampton, New York.

1926	Sage Hall, Dartmouth College, Hanover, Massachusetts.
1926–27	Annapolis roads development, Anne Arundel County, Maryland.
1926–32	Payne Whitney Gymnasium, Yale University, New Haven, Connecticut.
1927	Proposal for a bank and office building (unbuilt), New York.
1927	Brookwood (Frelinghuysen house), Far Hills, New Jersey.
1927	Woodend (Chester Wells house), Chevy Chase, Maryland.
1927	George Sicard house, Larchmont, New York.
1927	H. W. Lowe house, Wheatley Hills, New York.
1927	Proposed plan for Hunter College (unbuilt), New York (with Dwight James Baum).
1927	Proposal for War Memorial (unbuilt), Providence, Rhode Island.
1927	Roy D. Chapin house, Grosse Pointe, Michigan.
Begun 1927	Tuxedo Club, Tuxedo Park, New York.
1927–29	Junior League, New York.
1927–30	Hendricks Chapel, Syracuse University, Syracuse, New York.
1928	Gavin house, Long Island, New York.
1928	Villa Ospa, Jekyll Island, Georgia.
1928	Crane mausoleum, Chicago, Illinois.
1928	First Presbyterian Church, New Rochelle, New York.
1928	Proposal for the completion of Grant's Tomb (unbuilt), New York.
1928	Jacobs mausoleum, Baltimore, Maryland.
1928	Temple of the Scottish Rite, Baltimore, Maryland.
1928	The Waves (John Russell Pope house), Newport, Rhode Island.
1928–30	Spence School, New York.
1928–32	National City Christian Church, Washington, D.C.
1928–33	American Pharmaceutical Association building, Washington, D.C.
1929	Joseph J. Kerrigan estate, Oyster Bay, New York.
1929	Cincinnati Gas and Electric building, Cincinnati, Ohio.
1929	First Congregational Church, Columbus, Ohio.
1929	First National Bank of Mamaroneck, Mamaroneck, New York.
1929	Holy Trinity Church, The Bronx, New York.
1929	Proposed plan for Hartwick College (unbuilt), Oneonta, New York (with Dwight James Baum).
1929	Proposed wing (unbuilt), Metropolitan Museum of Art, New York.
1929	Proposal for Spouting Rock Beach Club, Newport, Rhode Island.
1929–31	Proposal for the Cloisters (unbuilt), New York.
1929–33	Calhoun College, Yale University, New Haven, Connecticut.
1929–37	Modern Sculpture Wing, Tate Gallery, London.
1929–39	Armor Hall, Metropolitan Museum of Art, New York.
1929–39	Elgin Marble Wing, British Museum, London.
c. 1930	Proposal for a movie studio (unbuilt).
c. 1930	Harold C. Richard apartment, New York.
1930	Virginia Graham Fair Vanderbilt house, New York.
1930	Proposal for George Rogers Clark Memorial (unbuilt), Vincennes, Indiana.
1930	Methodist Episcopal Church, Knoxville, Tennessee.
1930–32	E. P. Rogers estate, East Aurora, New York.
1930–33	National Archives, Washington, D.C.
c. 1931	Pavilions at Frick Park, Pittsburgh, Pennsylvania.
1931	Francis P. Garvan country house, Roslyn, New York.
1931	Garvan mausoleum, Woodlawn Cemetery, The Bronx, New York.
1931	Proposal for George Rogers Clark Memorial (unbuilt), Harrodsburg, Pennsylvania.
Begun 1931	Frick Collection, New York.
1931–37	Oscar Strauss Memorial, Washington, D.C. (completed 1947)
1932	Proposal for skyscraper (unbuilt), New York.
1932	Alpha Rho Chi Fraternity, Cornell University, Ithaca, New York.
1932	Laura Delano house, Rhinebeck, New York.
1932	Person Hall, University of North Carolina, Chapel Hill, North Carolina.
1932–40	Silliman College, Yale University, New Haven, Connecticut.
c. 1933	Post Office, Summit, New Jersey (with P. W. Burnham).
1933–35	Frick Art Reference Library, New York.
1934	Anthony Campagna estate, Riverdale, New York.
1934	Proposal for Art Institute of Chicago (unbuilt), Chicago, Illinois.
1934	Lawrence Farms, Mount Kisco, New York.
1934–36	United States Chancery, London.
c. 1935	Proposal for completion of American Museum of Natural History (unbuilt), New York.
c. 1935	Folger house, Washington, D.C.
1935	Proposal for Federal Reserve Board building (unbuilt), Washington, D.C.
1935	Galleries for Sir Joseph Duveen apartment, New York.
1935	Proposal for skyscraper (unbuilt), New York.
1935	Washington's Headquarters Museum, Morristown, New Jersey.
1935–37	Jefferson Memorial, Washington, D.C. (completed 1943)
1935–37	National Gallery of Art, Washington, D.C. (completed 1941)
c. 1936	Proposal for unidentified house (unbuilt).
1936	Louis Bertshman house, Syosset, New York.
1936–37	Dixie Plantation (Gerald Livingston house), Quitman, Georgia.
c. 1937	Proposal for Sir Joseph Duveen house (unbuilt), London.
1937	Proposal for Criminal Courts building (unbuilt), New York.

SELECTED BIBLIOGRAPHY

Books

Barber, Donn, ed. *Catalogue of the Twenty-Third Annual Exhibition of the Architectural League of New York.* New York: Architectural League, 1908.

Bergman, Edward F. *Woodlawn Remembers.* Utica, New York: North Country Books, 1988.

Brown, Glenn. *Memories 1860–1930.* Washington, D.C.: Glenn Brown, 1931.

Burchard, John, and Albert Bush-Brown. *The Architecture of America.* Boston: Little, Brown, 1961.

Carroll, Richard, ed. *Buildings and Grounds of Yale University.* New Haven: Yale University Printing Service, c. 1980.

Carson, Jeffrey, and Sue Kohler. *Sixteenth Street Architecture.* Washington, D.C.: Commission of Fine Arts, 1978.

Catalogue of the Annual Exhibition of the Department of Architecture, 1891. New York: Columbia College, 1891.

Catalogue of the Eighth Exhibition, Washington Architectural Club. Washington, D.C.: Washington Architectural Club, 1911.

Catalogue of the First Annual Exhibition of the American Academy in Rome. New York: American Academy in Rome, 1896.

Catalogue of the Thirty-Third Annual Exhibition of the Architectural League of New York. New York: Architectural League of New York, 1918.

Concklin, E. F. *The Lincoln Memorial in Washington.* Washington, D.C.: GPO, 1920.

Cortissoz, Royal. *The Architecture of John Russell Pope.* New York: Helburn, 1925–1930.

Cowdrey, Bartlett. *The National Academy of Design Exhibition Record 1826–1860.* New York: New York Historical Society, 1943.

Cram, Ralph Adams. *American Church Building of Today.* New York: Architectural Book Publishing Co., 1929.

Cremin, Lawrence. *American Education: The Metropolitan Experience, 1876–1980.* New York: Harper & Row, 1988.

De Penanrun, David, et al. *Les Architectes Elèves de L'Ecole des Beaux-Arts 1819–1907.* Paris: Guerinet, 1907.

D'Espouy, Hector. *Fragments d'Architecture Antique d'Apres les Releves et Restaurations des Ancients Pensionnaires de L'Academie de France a Rome.* Paris, 1905.

Egbert, Donald. *The Beaux-Arts Tradition in French Architecture.* Princeton: Princeton University Press, 1980.

Eggers, Otto R. *The American Architect Series of Early American Architecture.* New York: American Architect, 1922.

Embury, Aymar II. *One Hundred Country Houses.* New York: Century, 1909.

Les Esquissses d'Admission à L'Ecole Nationale et Spéciale des Beaux-Arts. Paris: Vincent, 1903.

Ferree, Barr. *Country Estates and Gardens.* New York: Munn, 1906.

Ferry, W. Hawkins. *The Buildings of Detroit.* Detroit: Wayne State University Press, 1968.

Finley, David E. *A Standard of Excellence: Andrew Mellon Founds the National Gallery of Art at Washington D.C.* Washington, D.C.: Smithsonian Press, 1973.

Francis, Dennis Steadman. *Architects in Practice in New York City 1900–1940.* New York: Copar, 1980.

Gibbs, Kenneth Turney. *Business Architectural Imagery in America, 1870–1930.* Ann Arbor, Michigan: University of Michigan Press, 1985.

Goode, James. *The Outdoor Sculpture of Washington, D.C.* Washington, D.C.: Smithsonian Institution Press, 1974.

Goodnow, Ruby Ross. *The Honest House.* New York: Century, 1914.

Goodwin, Phillip. *Built in the U.S.A.* New York: Museum of Modern Art, 1944.

Gréber, Jacques. *L'Architecture aux États-Unis.* Paris: Payot & Co., 1920.

Griffenhagen, George B. *The American Institute of Pharmacy: 50th Anniversary.* Washington, D.C.: American Pharmaceutical Association, 1984.

Guadet, Julien. *Eléments et Théorie de l'Architecture.* Paris: Librarie de la Construction Moderne, 1909.

Gurney, George. *Sculpture and the Federal Triangle*. Washington, D.C.: Smithsonian Press, 1985.

Gutheim, William. *Worthy of a Nation: The History of Planning for the National Capital*. Washington, D.C.: 1977.

Hamlin, Talbot Faulkner. *The American Spirit in Architecture*. New Haven: Yale University, 1926.

Herbert, William. *Houses for Town and Country*. New York: Duffield & Co., 1907.

Hewitt, Mark. *The Architect and the American Country House*. New Haven: Yale University Press, 1990.

Hill, Oliver, and Cornforth. *English Country Houses: Caroline, 1625–1685*. London: Country Life, 1966.

Hitchcock, Henry-Russell. *Architecture: Nineteenth and Twentieth Centuries*. 4th ed. New York: Penguin, 1977.

Hoak, et al. *Masterpieces of Architecture in the United States*. New York: Charles Scribner's Sons, 1930.

Howe, Samuel. *American Country Houses of Today 1915*. New York: Architectural Book Publishing, 1915.

Howe, Winifred E. *A History of the Metropolitan Museum of Art*. New York: Columbia University Press, 1946.

Hussey, Christopher. *English Country Houses: Mid-Georgian, 1760–1800*. London: Country Life, 1956.

Kaiser, Harvey. *Great Camps of Adirondacks*. Boston: David R. Godine, 1982.

Keefe, Charles. *The American House*. New York: U.P.C., 1922.

Kimball, Fiske, and George Edgell. *A History of Architecture*. New York: Harper and Brothers, 1918.

Klauder, Charles, and Herbert Wise. *College Architecture in America and Its Part in the Development of the Campus*. New York: Charles Scribner's Sons, 1929.

Knox, Katharine McCook. *The Story of the Frick Art Reference Library*. New York: Frick Art Reference Library, 1979.

Kohler, Sue A. *The Commission of Fine Arts, A Brief History 1910–1976, with Additions 1977–1984*. Washington, D.C.: Commission of Fine Arts, 1985.

Kohler, Sue, and Jeffrey Carson. *Massachusetts Avenue Architecture*. Washington, D.C.: Commission of Fine Arts, 1975.

Kopper, Philip. *America's National Gallery of Art: A Gift to the Nation*. New York: Abrams, 1991.

Kroker, Ernst. *Katechismus der Archaologie*. Leipzig: J. J. Weber, 1888.

Lampl, Paul. "Higgins, Daniel Paul." *Dictionary of American Biography*. New York: Charles Scribner's Sons, 1977.

Letarouilly, Paul. *Edifices de Rome Moderne*. Paris: Bance, 1856.

Levy, David. *Herbert Croly of the New Republic*. Princeton: Princeton University Press, 1985.

Lincoln Memorial Commission. *Lincoln Memorial Commission Report*. Washington: GPO, 1913.

Longstreth, Richard, ed. *The Mall in Washington, 1791–1991*. Washington, D.C.: National Gallery of Art, 1992.

Lowry, Bates. *Building a National Image*. Washington, D.C.: National Building Museum, 1985.

McKinzie, Richard. *The New Deal for Artists*. Princeton: Princeton University Press, 1973.

McNab, William R. *Residence of H. L. Dulin, Esq.* Knoxville, Tennessee: Dulin Gallery of Art, nd.

Les Medailles des Concours d'Architecture de L'Ecole Nationale des Beaux-Arts. Paris: Guerinet, 1910.

Milne, James Lees. *English Country Houses: Baroque, 1685–1715*. London: Country Life, 1968.

Mitchell, A. O. *Homes in the City and the Country*. New York: Charles A. Scribner's Sons, 1893.

Moore, Charles. *The Life and Times of Charles Follen McKim*. Boston: Houghton Mifflin, 1929.

Morgan, Keith. *Charles A. Platt*. New York: Architectural History Foundation, 1985.

Mosenthal, P. J. *The City College*. New York: Putnam's, 1907.

Mumford, Lewis. *Sticks and Stones*. New York: 1924.

Naylor, Maria. *The National Academy of Design Exhibition Record 1861–1900*. New York: Kennedy Gallery, 1973.

Octagon Building Committee. *The Octagon*. Washington D.C.: AIA, 1927.

Oliver, Richard, ed. *The Making of an Architect*. New York: Rizzoli, 1981.

Osborn, H. F. *History Plan and Design of the New York State Roosevelt Memorial*. New York: American Museum of Natural History, 1928.

Paris, William F., ed. *Hall of American Artists: Personalities on American Art*. New York: W. F. Paris, 1951.

Patterson, Augusta Owen. *American Homes of Today*. New York: MacMillan, 1924.

Pindar, George. *The New York State Theodore Roosevelt Memorial*. New York: American Museum of Natural History, 1936.

Plattsburgh Centenary Commission, *Dedication of the Thomas Macdonough Memorial*. Plattsburgh, New York: 1926.

Pope, John Russell. *Campus Plans*. New York: Helburn, 1925.

Pope, John Russell. *Report of the Architect on Designs Submitted for a Lincoln Memorial on the Meridian Hill Site and on the Soldiers' Home Grounds Site*. New York: John Russell Pope, 1912.

Pope, John Russell. *Yale University, a Plan for its Future Building*. New York: John Russell Pope, 1919.

Post, Edwin. *Truly Emily Post*. New York: Funk & Wagnall's, 1961.

Public Buildings Commission. *Public Buildings in the District of Columbia*. Washington, D.C.: GPO, 1918.

Robinson, Sidney, and Richard Guy Wilson, eds. *Modern Architecture in America: Visions and Revisions*. Ames, Iowa: Iowa State University Press, 1991.

Roosevelt Memorial Association. *Plan and Design for the Roosevelt Memorial in the City of Washington: John Russell Pope, Architect*. New York: Pynchon Press, 1925.

Rorimer, James J. *The Cloisters*. New York: Metropolitan Museum of Art, 1939.

Scott, Fred W. *Royal Orchard: Freddie's History 1902–1978*. Richmond: privately printed, 1979.

Sexton, R. M. *American Commercial Buildings of Today*. New York: Architectural Book Publishing Co., 1928.

———, ed. *American Public Buildings of Today*. New York: Architectural Book Publishing Co., 1930.

Seymour, Charles. *Yale Residential Colleges*. New Haven: Yale Publishing Association, 1933.

Snyder, Frank M. *Building Details*. New York: Frank Snyder, 1907.

Stern, Robert, et al. *New York 1900*. New York: Rizzoli, 1983.

Turner, Paul Venable. *Campus: An American Planning Tradition*. New York: MIT Press, 1984.

Valentine, Lucia, and Alan Valentine. *The American Academy in Rome 1894–1969*. Charlottesville: University of Virginia Press, 1973.

Van Zanten, David. *Designing Paris*. Cambridge: MIT Press, 1987.

Ward, James. *Architects in Practice in New York: 1900–1940*. New York: J & D Associates, 1989.

Ware, William Robert. *The American Vignola*. Scranton, Pennsylvania: International Textbook Co., 1905.

Wilson, Diana G. *The Mausoleum of Henry and Arabella Huntington*. San Marino, California: Huntington Museum, 1989.

Wright and Parks, eds. *The History of History in American Schools of Architecture 1865–1975*. New York: Princeton Architectural Press, 1990.

Year Book of the Architectural League of New York and Catalogue of the Forty-Fourth Annual Exhibition. New York: Architectural League, 1929.

Periodicals

"Address Delivered by Waddy B. Wood to the Association of Federal Architects." *Federal Architect* 2 (July 1931): 12.

"American Country House Architecture." *Town & Country* 63 (9 May 1908): 32.

"American Country Houses: The Residence of Andrew V. Stout, Esq." *Country Life* 39 (March 1921): 69.

"American Homes: Some Domestic Work by John Russell Pope." *Architectural Review* 53 (March/April 1923): 77–85, 120–25.

"Architecture of American Colleges II: Yale." *Architectural Record* 26 (December 1909): 393–416.

"Architecture of American Colleges VI: Dartmouth, Williams and Amherst." *Architectural Record* 28 (December 1910): 424–42.

"Archives Building." *Federal Architect* 5 (July 1934): np.

Aslet, Clive. "America's Winter Newport: Jekyll Island Georgia." Parts 1 and 2. *Country Life* (27 September 1984): 834–37; (4 October 1984): 947–50.

Bartlett, Stuart. "Some Newport Villas." *The Architectural Review* 15 (March 1908): 35–53.

"'Bonniecrest,' An example of Noble Architecture for the Country Home." *Craftsman* 29 (January 1916): 14–24.

Bottomley, W. L. "The American Country House." *Architectural Record* 48 (October 1920): 258–368.

Boyd, John Taylor Jr. "Otto R. Eggers, Architectural Renderer & Designer." *Architectural Record* 43 (May 1918): 421–27.

———. "The Residence of the Honorable Henry White." *Architectural Record* 42 (November 1917): 402–19.

Brown, Glenn. "The Artistic Growth of the Washington Plan" *Architectural Record* 59 (April 1926): 311–25.

———. "The Lincoln Memorial In Washington, D.C." Parts 1 and 2. *American Architect* 118 (20 October 1920): 489–506; (27 October 1920): 523–39.

———. "Roosevelt Memorial Site." *Architectural Record* 60 (December 1926): 587–88

Bryant, Keith. "Cathedrals, Castles and Roman Baths: Railway Station Architecture in the Urban South." *Journal of Urban History* 2 (February 1976): 195–230.

"Calhoun College, Yale University." *Architectural Forum* 60 (May 1934): 321–30.

Capitol Commission. "Nebraska State Capitol Competition,." *American Architect* 118 (21 July 1920): 79–80.

Chamberlain, Samuel. "An Appreciation of the Renderings of Otto R. Eggers, Architect." *American Architect* 127 (15 July 1925): 39–41.

Childs, Marquis. "Mr. Pope's Memorial." *Magazine of Art* 30 (April 1937): 200–202.

"Cleveland Public Library." *Architecture* 35 (April 1917): plates 56–58.

"Competition tor a Building tor the Federal Reserve Board." *Architectural Forum* 63 (July 1935): 6–9.

"Competition for the New York State Roosevelt Memorial." *American Architect* 128 (1 July 1925): 14.

"Constitution Hall of the D.A.R., Washington, D.C." *Architecture* 70 (July 1934): 13–22.

Cortissoz, Royal. "The American School of Architecture in Rome," *Harper's Weekly* 39 (15 June 1895): 564–65.

"Country Club, Tuxedo, New York." *American Architect* 131 (5 March 1927): 278.

"Country Houses of Character." *Country Life* 37 (November 1919): 24–30.

"Country Life in America, No. 3: Skylands Farm, the New Jersey Estate of Clarence Lewis." *Country Life* 72 (August 1937): 34–41.

Croly, Herbert. "The Farmhouse 'Deluxe': Country Seat of Robert J. Collier, Esq." *Architectural Record* 31 (June 1912): 561–74.

———. "A New Use of Old Forms, Two Houses by John Russell Pope." *Architectural Record* 17 (April 1905): 271–93.

———. "Recent Works of John Russell Pope." *Architectural Record* 29 (June 1911): 441–511.

———. "The Stuart Duncan Residence at Newport." *Architectural Record* 38 (September 1915): 289–309.

Delano, William A. "Memoirs of Centurian Architects." Parts 1 and 2. *Journal of the A.I.A.* 10 (July–August 1948): 3–9; 81–87.

Eggers, Otto R. "The Genesis of a Rendering." *Pencil Points* 3 (November 1922): 10–13, 35.

Embury, Aymar. "Are We on Our Way?" *Arts and Decoration* 14 (January 1921): 284–85.

"Enduring Dignity." *Country Life* 76 (September 1939): 23–25.

"Episcopal Church at Westbury, Long Island," *Brickbuilder* 24 (December 1915): 301–04.

"First Design in the Journal's New Series of Model Suburban Houses Which Can Be Built at Moderate Cost." *Ladies' Home Journal* 17 (October 1900): 15.

"First Presbyterian Church." *Architectural Forum* 63 (August 1935): 99–107.

"Flexibility, Simplicity and Accessibility." *Architectural Forum* 61 (September 1934): 197–201.

"Forty-second Annual Exhibition of the Architectural League of New York." *American Architect* 131 (5 March 1927): 269–80.

"George Rogers Clark Memorial Competition." *Pencil Points* 11 (April 1930): 293–95.

"Georgian House." *American Architect* 117 (7 January 1920): 5–6.

Gillespie, Harriet Sisson. "A Superb Replica of Historic Tudor Type." *Arts and Decoration* 25 (May 1926): 44–47, 96.

Githens, Alfred Morton. "The Group Plan, I–V." *Brickbuilder* 15 (August 1906): 134–39, 179–82; 16 (December 1906): 154–57, 185–87, 219–25.

Greenfield, Kent Roberts. "The Museum: Its First Half Century." *Baltimore Museum of Art Annual* 1 (1966): 5–35.

Grieg, James. "New Sculpture Halls for the National Gallery, Millbank." *London Studio* 114 (July 1937): 139, 141.

Grossman, Elizabeth G. "Architecture for a Public Client: The Monuments and Chapels of the American Battle Monuments Commission." *Journal of the Society of Architectural Historians* 43 (May 1984): 119–43.

———. "Two Postwar Competitions: The Nebraska State Capitol and the Kansas City Liberty Memorial." *Journal of the Society of Architectural Historians* 45 (September 1986): 244–69.

"Hartwick College." *Architect* 13 (November 1929): 152, 154.

"Henry Barton Jacobs' Newport Home." *Architecture* 11 (April 1905): plates 35–38.

Herkalo, Keith A. "The Citizens' Revolt that shaped City Hall." *North Country Notes* 293 (January 1993): 2.

Hitchcock, Henry-Russell. "Our Domestic Architecture." *Town & Country* 100 (December 1946): 99–116.

"House of Commodore Charles A. Gould Greenlawn, Long Island." *American Architect* 109 (19 January 1916): 38–40.

"House of Reginald DeKoven." *Brickbuilder* 22 (June 1913): plates 81–82.

"House of Stuart Duncan." *American Architect* 108 (22 September 1915): 193–203.

Howard, John Galen. "The Outlook and In Look Architectural," *Architectural Record* 43 (September 1912): 531–42.

Howe, Samuel. "Architecture of the Tudors in America's Metropolis—Mr. Reginald De Koven's Recent Addition to Park Avenue." *Arts and Decoration* 3 (July 1913): 302–304.

———. "A Dramatic and Virile Portrayal of a Medieval Theme." *Arts and Decoration* 6 (January 1916): 125–29.

———. "Mrs. Henry Barton Jacobs' Newport Home." *Town & Country* 68 (10 May 1913): 43–45.

Hudnut, Joseph. "The Last of the Romans." *Magazine of Art* 34 (April 1941): 169–73.

———. "Twilight of the Gods." *Magazine of Art* 30 (August 1937): 480–524.

"Hunter College Plan." *Architect* 8 (September 1927): 710.

"Interiors of the Marshall Field Residence." *Country Life* 52 (September 1927): 49–56.

"Jacksonville Terminal Competition." *American Architect* 110 (4 October 1916): plates.

"Jefferson Memorial." *New Republic* 90 (7 April 1937): 265–66.

"John Russell Pope." *Pencil Points* 18 (October 1937): 48, 50.

"John Russell Pope Appointed Architect of the New York

State Roosevelt Memorial." *Architecture* 52 (July 1925): 257–58.

"Kamp Kill Kare." *Country Life* 45 (December 1923): 57–58.

Kimball, Fiske. "The American Country House." *Architectural Record* 46 (October 1919): 291–400.

———. "John Russell Pope 1874–1937." *American Architect and Architecture* 151 (October 1937): 87.

Lescaze, William. "America is Outgrowing Imitation Greek Architecture." *Magazine of Art* 30 (June 1937): 366–69.

Leuchak, Mary Rebecca. "'The Old World and the New': Developing the Design for the Cloisters." *Metropolitan Journal* 23 (1988): 257–76.

"Lincoln Memorial: The Man and the Monument." *The Craftsman* 26 (April 1914): 16–20.

"Marcus L. Ward Home for Aged and Respectable Bachelors and Widowers, Maplewood, N.J." *American Architect* 127 (11 March 1925): 204–14.

"Macdonough Memorial." *Architectural Forum* 46 (December 1926): plate 97.

McCready, E. S. "The Nebraska State Capitol: Its Design, Background and Influence." *Nebraska History* 55 (Fall 1974).

McMillan, James. "The American Academy in Rome." *The North American Review* 174 (May 1902): 627.

"Memorial to Theodore Roosevelt in Washington, D.C." *American Architect* 130 (20 May 1926): plates 105–108.

"Monographs on Architectural Renderers I: The Work of Otto R. Eggers." *The Brickbuilder* 23 (January 1914): 7–9.

"Montfaucon Memorial." *The Architect* 8 (May 1927): 188.

Mumford, Lewis. "The Sky Line: Unconscious Architecture." *The New Yorker* 7 (13 February 1932): 46, 48.

"National City Christian Church, Washington, D.C." *Architecture* 70 (November 1934): 251–56.

"Nebraska State Capitol." *American Architect* 118 (21 and 28 July 1920): plates.

"New York Junior League Clubhouse." *The Architect* 12 (July 1929): 380, 382.

"New York State Roosevelt Memorial Competition." *Architectural Forum* 43 (July 1925): 9–10.

"Newark Memorial Competition." *American Architect* 110 (11 October 1916): plates 233, 240.

O'Neal, William B. "The Multiple Life of Space." *Arts in Virginia* 5 (Spring 1965): 1–13.

Paris, William F. "John Russell Pope." *Hall of American Artists* 6 (1951): 31.

Patterson, Augusta Owen. "The Residence of Mr. and Mrs. Marshall Field." *Town & Country* 82 (15 August 1927): 35–46.

"Payne Whitney Gymnasium and Ray Tompkins House." *Architectural Record* 73 (February 1933): 74–104.

"Plattsburg City Hall." *Architectural Forum* 33 (December 1920): plates 85–88.

Pope, Arthur Upham. "Defending the Jefferson Memorial." *New Republic* 91 (12 May 1937): 20–21.

———. "In Defense of the Jefferson Memorial." *Magazine of Art* 30 (June 1937): 363–65.

Pope, John Russell. "The Complete Country Estate I—The House and Farm Buildings." *Country Life* 38 (October 1920): 35–40.

Price, C. Matlack. "The Development of a National Architecture 1–5." *Arts and Decoration* 2–3 (November 1911–September 1913).

———. "'Meridian House': Residence of Irwin Laughlin, Esq." *Architectural Record* 51 (August 1929): 223–228.

———. "A Study in Country Architecture." *International Studio* 48 (November 1912): xii–xiii.

———. "The Wherefore of Good Architecture." *Arts and Decoration* 14 (April 1921): 435–40.

"Prize Winning Design—Competition for a Memorial to Theodore Roosevelt in Washington, D.C." *American Architect* 129 (20 January 1926): plates 7–10.

"Program of a Competition for the Selection of an Architect for a Fountain to be Erected near the entrance to Central Park." *American Competitions* 3 (1913): xxxiii, plates 146–49.

"Providence War Memorial." *The Architect* 8 (September 1927): 704–06.

"Residence of Clarence McK. Lewis, Esq., Sterlington, NY." *Architectural Forum* 54 (February 1931): 185–215.

"Residence of Reginald DeKoven." *Architectural Record* 42 (August 1917): 153–162.

"Robert H. McCormick House." *Architectural Review* (Boston) 21 (August, 1916): plates 105–112 and 75–77.

"Robert Low Bacon, Jr., House." *American Architect* 117 (31 March 1920): 397–403.

"Roosevelt Memorial Site." *Architectural Record* 60 (December 1926): 587–88.

"Sage Hall." *Architect* 7 (October 1926): plates 1–4.

Smith, Howard Dwight. "Furniture and Decoration in Monumental Buildings; Temple of the Scottish Rite, Washington, D.C." *Good Furniture* 9 (September 1917): 207–24.

———. "The New Passenger Railway Station at Richmond, Virginia." *Architectural Review* 8 (June 1919): 147–62.

———. "Recent Domestic Architecture from the Designs of John Russell Pope." *The Brickbuilder* 35 (August 1916): 189–204.

———. "The Relation of the House to the Landscape." *The American Architect* 113 (3 April 1918): 397–404.

Stanton, Phoebe. "A Note on John Russell Pope." *Baltimore Museum of Art Annual* 4 (1972): 60–69.

Swales, Francis S. "Master Draftsmen VIII, John Russell Pope." *Pencil Points* 5 (December 1924): 65–80, 90.

Taylor, Margaret Shaw. "The New Club House of the New York Junior League." *Architectural Forum* 53 (July 1930): 1–6.

"Temple of the Scottish Rite." *Architectural Review* 4 (January 1916): entire issue.

"Union Passenger Station." *American Architect and Building News.* 96 (9 July 1919): 33.

"University Baptist Church." *Pencil Points* 7 (August 1926): color supplement.

"University Club, Milwaukee Wis." *American Architect* 129 (5 June 1926): Plates 122–24.

Van Horn, Henry. "A French Shooting-Box on Long Island Hills." *Town & Country* 71 (1 January 1916): 20–21.

———. "A Very Personal Adaptation of the Georgian." *Town & Country* 72 (10 September 1916): 17–21.

Van Zanten, David. "Le Système des Beaux-Arts." *Architecture d'Aujourd'hui* 182 (December 1975): 97–106.

"Westbury Chapel." *American Architect* 122 (13 September 1922): 232, 241, and plates.

"What are the Outstanding Buildings?" *Federal Architect* 2 (April 1932): 10.

Whitehead, Russell. "A House at Greenwich, Conn." *Architectural Record* 49 (April 1921): 297–98.

Wines, Roger. "Vanderbilt's Motor Parkway: America's First Auto Road." *Journal of Long Island History* 2 (Fall 1962): 14–28.

Wood, Waddy. "A House of Unusual Architectural Merit." *The Brickbuilder* 22 (February 1913): 27–32.

"Working Photographs." *American Architect and Building News* 125 (27 February 1925): 197–99.

Young, T. J. "Otto Eggers as a Designer." *Pencil Points* 18 (November 1937): 683–714.

Other Sources

American Battle Monuments Commission. *Annual Report of the American Battle Monuments Commission*, Washington, D.C.: GPO, 1926.

American Institute of Architects Archives, Washington, D.C. Files listed as Competitions 1921–1935. Secretary's files. Correspondence files.

American Museum of Natural History Archives, Washington, D.C. President's files. Drawing Collection.

Architectural League of New York. Exhibition records compiled by Dennis Francis.

Archives Nationales, Paris. *Feuille de Valeurs 4840*, John Russell Pope. *Procés-Verbaux, 10 Jan. 1893 –19 Oct. 1897.*

British Museum Archives, London. Minutes of the Standing Committee.

Bushong, William. "Glenn Brown, The American Institute of Architects, and the Development of the Civic Core of Washington." Ph.D. diss., George Washington University, 1988.

College of the City of New York Archives, New York. Fraternity records (transcripts, handbooks, alumni files, and catalogues).

Columbia University, New York. Central files.

Columbia University, Avery Library Archives, New York. Edwin R. Will Collection. McKim, Mead & White Collection. Photograph Collection. Ware Collection. Gottscho Collection.

Columbia University, Butler Library, New York. Rare Books and Manuscripts Collection. Henry White Papers.

Carnegie Museum, Pittsburgh. Garvan house drawings.

Cleveland Public Library Archives, Cleveland. Building competition files.

Dartmouth College Archives, Hanover, Massachusetts. Campus planning files.

Daughters of the American Revolution Archives, Washington, D.C. Secretary-General's Papers.

Division of Historic Preservation, New York State Parks and Recreation Department, Albany, New York. Building survey files.

Eisenhower Library, Abilene, Kansas. Presidents' Papers, 1929 to 1930.

Frick Art Reference Library, New York. Photographic files. Royal Cortissoz's newspaper clipping files.

Graybill, Samuel H. "Bruce Price, American Architect." Ph.D. diss., Yale University, 1957.

Hartwick College Archives, Oneonta, New York. Campus planning files.

Henry E. Huntington Library and Art Gallery, San Marino, California. Henry E. Huntington Papers.

The Johns Hopkins University, Ferdinand Hamburger Jr. Archives, Baltimore.

The Johns Hopkins University Hospital Archives, Baltimore. Dr. Henry Barton Jacobs Papers.

Library of Congress, Manuscript Division, Washington, D.C. Charles McKim Papers. Charles Moore Papers. William Howard Taft Papers. Warren Harding Papers. David Finley Papers.

Library of Congress, Prints and Photographs Division. Historic American Building Survey. Washingtoniana Collection. Copyright filing material. Samuel Gottscho Collection.

Lincoln Birthplace National Historic Site, National Park Service, Hodgenville Kentucky. Site files. Records of the Lincoln Memorial Birthplace Association.

Massachusetts Institute of Technology Archives, Cambridge, Massachusetts. William Robert Ware Collection.

National Archives, Washington, D.C. Records of the Lincoln Memorial Commission, RG 42. Department of the Interior Records, RG 48. Records of the National Archives, RG 64. Commission of Fine Arts Files and Minutes, RG 66. Charles Moore, unpublished autobiography. Records of the Public Buildings Commission, Board of Architectural Consultants, RG 121. Records of the Foreign Building Office, Department of State Records. District of Columbia Records, RG 351.

National Commission of Fine Arts. *Eleventh Report of the National Commission of Fine Arts.* Washington, D.C.: GPO, 1930.

National Commission of Fine Arts. *Tenth Report of the National Commission of Fine Arts.* Washington, D.C.: GPO, 1926.

National Gallery of Art Archives, Washington, D.C. Drawing and Newspaper Clipping Collections. David Finley Papers.

New York City Landmarks Preservation Commission, New York. Files.

Office of the Architect of the Capitol, Washington, D.C. Lincoln Memorial files.

Plattsburgh City Clerk's Office, Plattsburgh, New York. Minutes of the Plattsbugh City Hall Commission.

Richmond, Fredericksburg and Potomac Railroad Archives, Richmond, Virginia. Newspaper clipping files.

Rockefeller Archive Center, Pocantico Hills, New York. John D. Rockefeller Papers. Rockefeller Family Archives, RG 2. Papers of Office the Messrs. Rockefeller, RG 2. Rockefeller Family Business Interests.

Roosevelt Presidential Library, Hyde Park, New York. Franklin D. Roosevelt diaries, personal papers, office files.

Seventh Annual Report of the Board of Trustees of the New York State Roosevelt Memorial. New York: American Museum of Natural History, 1931.

Smithsonian Institution, Archives of American Art, Washington, D.C. Francis Patrick Garvan Papers. American Academy in Rome Papers.

Smithsonian Institution, Office of Research Support, Washington, D.C. Peter Juley Collection.

Sterling and Francine Clarke Art Institute, Williamstown, Massachusetts. Duveen Collection.

Tate Gallery Archives, London. Trustees' Minutes.

Textile Museum, Washington, D.C. George Hewitt Myers Papers.

Theodore Roosevelt Birthplace National Historic Site, New York. Theodore Roosevelt Memorial Association Papers.

Tompkins, Sally Kress. "The Quest for Grandeur: Charles Moore, the Commission of Fine Arts, and the Federal Triangle." Master's thesis, George Washington University, 1976.

Townsend, Gavin. "The Tudor House in America." Ph.D. diss., University of California at Santa Barbara, 1986.

University of Virginia, Alderman Library, Charlottesville, Virginia. Fiske Kimball Papers. Judge Howard Smith Collection.

U.S. Congress, Committee on the Library, House of Representatives. *Hearing Before the Committee on the Library, House of Representatives on H.J. Res. 217, a Joint Resolution Providing for the Construction and Maintenance of a National Gallery of Art.* Washington, D.C.: GPO, 1937.

U.S. Congress, Committee on the Library, House of Representatives. *Site for the Jefferson Memorial; Hearing Before the Committee on the Library, House of Representatives.* Washington, D.C.: GPO, 1937.

U.S. Congress, Senate Committee on the District of Columbia. *The Improvement of the Park System of the District of Columbia.* S. Rept. 166, 57th Cong., 1st sess. Washington, D.C.: GPO, 1902.

U.S. Senate. *Designs, Plans, and Suggestions for the Aggrandisement of Washington.* Washington, D.C.: GPO, 1900.

Valentine Museum, Richmond, Virginia. Cook Collection.

Virginia Historic Landmarks Commission, Richmond, Virginia. Building survey files.

Washington National Records Center, Suitland, Maryland. Records of the American Battle Monuments Commission, RG 117. Records of the Public Buildings Commission, RG 121.

Wilmington Public Library, Wilmington, North Carolina. Local history files.

Yale University Archives, New Haven, Connecticut. Minutes of the Meetings of the Yale Corporation, 1916–1919. Papers of the Office of the Secretary. Yale Corporation's Committee on Architectural Plan. Carroll Meeks Papers. Papers of President James Angell. Provosts' Papers.

Yale University, Beinecke Library, New Haven, Connecticut. Royal Cortissoz Papers.

INDEX